BARCODE
ON NEXT
PAGE ·

D1162766

AW 2017

3 1160 00213 3168

2012 onlycopy
MEL

AUTOGIRO

The Story of
"the Windmill Plane"

Dedication

Every book should be dedicated to someone. No author completes an entire manuscript without a special person kissing him on the forehead, putting his pencil or typewriter in his hand and saying, "C'mon, Bustah, do at least another chapter." I have to thank Sissy, who urged, threatened, begged, pleaded and encouraged me to finally complete twenty years' work.

George Townson

AUTOGIRO

The Story of "the Windmill Plane"

By George Townson

AERO PUBLISHERS, INC.
329 West Aviation Road, Fallbrook, CA 92028

Copyright © 1985 by George Townson. All Rights Reserved. Printed in the United States of America. No part of this publication may be reproduced, stored in a retrieval system, or transmitted, in any form or by any means, electronic, mechanical, photocopying, recording, or otherwise, without prior written permission.

Library of Congress Cataloging in Publication Data
Townson, George.
    Autogiro: the windmill plane.
    Includes index.
    1. Autogiros—History. I. Title.
TL715.T69   1985   629.133'35   85-7538
ISBN 0-8168-2900-4

PRINTED AND BOUND IN THE UNITED STATES OF AMERICA

FOREWORD

AUTOGIRO is a comprehensive book portraying the development work of the Autogiro Company of America and its licensees during the period 1928 through 1943. The book gives details on the design, various methods of construction and flight characteristics of each model of autogiro that was produced and test flown during the period. The text is complemented by numerous photographs and 3-view scale drawings.

It is fortunate that the most qualified person to write this book actually was inspired to take on the task. George Townson's unique qualifications can be separated into three areas: Pilot, Mechanic and Engineer.

George was first fascinated by flight when he saw the Army "Round the World" fly over his home in suburban Philadelphia. At the age of 15, he began working on airplanes and two years later, in 1932, soloed in an Aeronca C3. He obtained his private license in 1932 and his commercial license at the age of 20 in an OX-5 powered KR-31 "Challenger." George continued his training and obtained an Instructor's rating in fixed-wing aircraft, gyroplanes and helicopters. In 1936, he was test pilot for the Herrick Convertaplane, which could be flown as a fixed-wing biplane, as a gyroplane and could be converted in flight to a rotary-wing type by releasing the upper wing to rotate. Over 100 in-flight air conversions were made. The Herrick Convertaplane now resides in the Air and Space National Museum facility in Silver Hill, Maryland.

In 1938 and 1939, George was engaged in crop-dusting with a Pitcairn PCA-2 Autogiro and shortly thereafter was hired as Piasecki's test pilot to fly the PV-2 helicopter and the Navy XHRP.1, the world's largest helicopter in 1944. During World War II, George was an instructor in the CPT Civilian Pilot Training Program, instructing in the Waco UPF and later flew evaluation tests for the United States Air Force on two unpowered rotorkites to determine the feasibility of towing helicopters to extend their range.

In 1946, George assisted in the building and test flew a light tandem-rotor, two-place helicopter at the Boulevard Airport in Philadelphia. In 1958, he worked with Kellett Aircraft acting as assistant project engineer and experimental test pilot during the rebirth of the Kellett KD-1A autogiro. George continues to hold a valid pilot's license and has now flown over 6000 hours in 250 various models of aircraft, including nine makes and models of helicopters and eight various models of gyroplanes.

Early in his flying career, George completed his training as an aircraft mechanic and received both the A & E and IA ratings. He has owned his own maintenance shop and maintained and overhauled both liquid cooled and air cooled engines ranging in horsepower from 27 hp. to 1300 hp. Some of the more bizarre engines with which George has had experience are: Jacobs, Anzani, Liberty, Curtiss "Conqueror," LeBlonde, Szekely, Wright J5, etc. The list of aircraft maintained, overhauled and restored by George is too long to recite here but I am sure he has worked on most every aircraft in the alphabet between Aeronca and Waco. During his career in aircraft maintenance, George has held many positions, the more notable being:

Customer Training Maintenance Engineer—
Boeing Vertol

Maintenance Supervisor and Special Projects
Manager, Altair Airlines

Instructor in all aspects of engine and airframe
maintenance including sheet metal, welding,
woodworking, fabric covering, painting,
rigging, etc.

Author of many technical and maintenance articles
which have been published in national trade
magazines.

Earlier, I mentioned George's qualifications as an engineer. Although George does not have an aeronautical engineering degree, he has the inquisitive mind of an engineer and is able to analyze a technical problem and come up with a practical solution. He understands the aerodynamics of both fixed-wing and rotary-wing aircraft and has built from scratch several airplanes and one helicopter.

George is a member of many aviation clubs and societies, including the Aviation/Space Writers Association. I think, however, he is most proud of his membership in the Society of Experimental Test Pilots.

"Autogiro" takes the reader through the development of the autogiro in the United States and portrays the magnitude of the engineering problems that had to be solved by creative engineering and trial and error in the flight testing programs. The culmination of this early pioneer work in the autogiro development led to the emergence of the first practical helicopter in the late 1930s and mid-1940s.

I am pleased that I was given the opportunity to tell the reader a little bit about George's vast and practical background in aviation which makes him eminently qualified to author this book.

Several years ago, when I was searching, without success, for an older and experienced mechanic to work for me in restoring a Pitcairn PCA-2 Autogiro and Pitcairn Mailwing, George's position with Altair Airlines was terminated by bankruptcy of the Company and George agreed to work for me as an independent contractor.

At this writing, George Townson is still very much involved in continuing his career in the areas of mechanical and engineering expertise. Depicted on the back cover in 1984 the Champion Spark Plug PCA-2 Pitcairn Autogiro which the author personally restored to flight condition over a two and one-half year period. In addition to the PCA-2, George is now restoring a Kellett K2 and a Pitcairn PA-7 Mailwing.

Stephen Pitcairn

INTRODUCTION

When the autogiro first appeared in the U.S., the News Media called it a "windmill plane." Although it did resemble a windmill the principle by which it flew is just the opposite of the reason that a windmill rotates. The blades or vanes of a windmill are PUSHED around by the air that passes through. In other words they follow the air. The blades of the autogiro rotor turn INTO the air. A delicate balance of the forces of lift and drag produce a force that PULLS the blade forward. The phenomenon is called AUTOROTATION. The engine of the Autogiro was not connected to the rotor in flight. It only pulled the craft through the air for takeoff and climb.

Sr. Juan de la Cierva   *(Pitcairn Photo)*

The inventor of the autogiro was Juan de la Cierva who did most of his development work in Spain. His first successful flight was made at Getafe Airdome in Spain, January 9, 1923. The word autogiro was coined by Cierva. It was initially a proprietary word and trademark. Random House dictionary showed autogiro spelled with a capital "A" to be given to craft built by Cierva or his followers. When spelled without the capital it referred to craft which flew with unpowered rotors.

During the course of his work he licensed most of the prominent aircraft manufacturers in Europe to build autogiros under his patents. Harold Pitcairn, builder of the famous Pitcairn Mailwing, obtained a license to build and develop the autogiro in the United States and to sublicense other manufacturers. This is the point at which this story begins.

First flight of the Cierva Autogiro at Getaffe Airport in Madrid Spain. Gomez Spencer, Pilot, January 9, 1923.

(Cierva Photo)

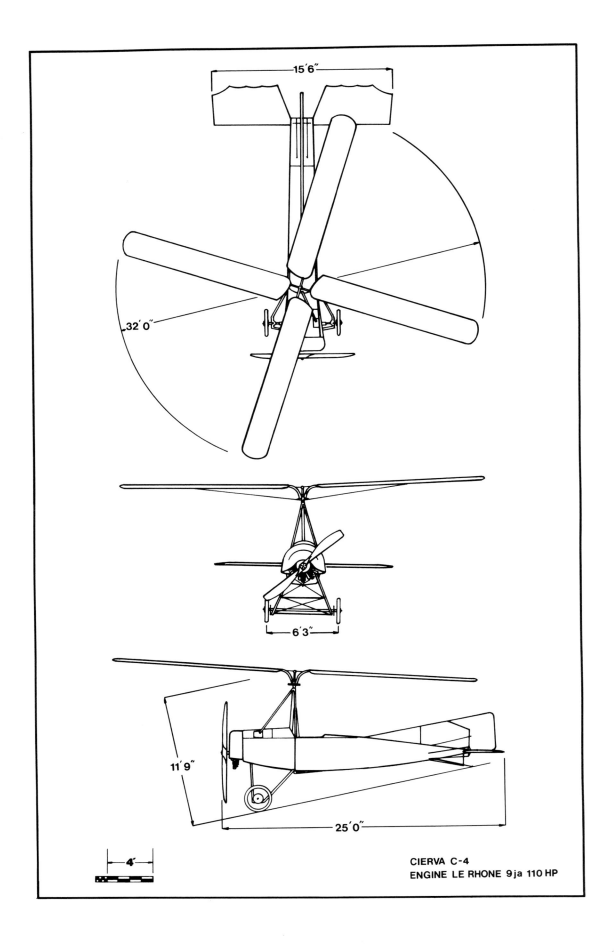

15'6"

32'0"

6'3"

11'9"

25'0"

4'

CIERVA C-4
ENGINE LE RHONE 9ja 110 HP

ACKNOWLEDGEMENTS

It takes a lot of research to compile a history such as this. Through the more than twenty years that I have been putting it all together the following organizations and individuals have come forward with photographs and data to make it all possible.

National Air and Space Museum
National Archives
Pitcairn Aviation
Kellett Corporation
Stephen Pitcairn
Garl Gunther
Ralph McClarren
John Underwood
Bill Hannan

Warren Ship
Howard Levy
Charles Gilfillan
Elsworth Thompson
DuPont Graphic Arts
Driscol A. Nina
A. W. Bayer
Joe Juptner

Some of the material used in the section, "The theory and discussion of the autogiro" was prepared originally for AOPA *Pilot* magazine.

ABOUT THE PHOTOGRAPHS:

Researchers handle and view many hundreds of photographs in the course of their research. The photographers are often not identified. Photo services may no longer be in business, or the photographer may be deceased.

Some of the photographs in AUTOGIRO are known to be made by Underwood and Underwood, Acme, Alfred DiLardi, Aero Service, Dalin Aerial Surveys. Others are from collections of Pitcairn Co., Kellett, National Archives, The Smithsonian Institution, John Underwood, Warren Ship, Howard Levy, Driscol A. Nina, Bill Hannan, Ellsworth Thompson, A.W. Bayer, and the Author.

Three-view drawings by Mark Mancini.

TABLE OF CONTENTS

A "gaggle" of autogiros, PAA-2 at top and five Pitcairn PCA-2 Autogiros below. (Pitcairn Photo)

Pitcairn Takes the Autogiro

Cierva C-8 Autogiro with American Wright J-5 9 cylinder aircooled 220 Hp radial engine replacing the usual 180 Hp "Viper" engine. Notice, no turned-up wing tips, yet. Insert: Harold F. Pitcairn, Founder of Pitcairn Aviation, Pitcairn Autogiro Company and Autogiro Company of America.

(Pitcairn Photo)

Harold Pitcairn of Bryn Athyn, a suburb of Philadelphia, Pennsylvania, began experimenting with helicopters in 1923. He worked hard at overcoming the problem of counteracting the torque caused by the rotor. He obtained at least one patent for devices to offset the torque. Working with him was a close friend, Agnew Larsen. Some time earlier, Pitcairn had wanted to form a company with Larsen as Chief Engineer. Larsen declined, saying that he lacked the all-round experience, instead he joined the famous Thomas-Morse Company working under B. D. Thomas. Larsen told the writer during an interview that he had taken a verbal trouncing from Thomas when Thomas-Morse lost the production contract for the Thomas-Morse MB-3 fighter to the Boeing Company. Ironically, when Larsen made the detail production drawings of the MB-3 for the Signal Corps, he did such an excellent job that, using these drawings, Boeing was able to out-bid Thomas-Morse for building Thomas-Morse's own design.

In February of 1925, Pitcairn and Larsen left for a twelve-week tour of Europe. The tour included Britain, France and Germany as well as Spain. On this trip the duo was not able to see

the autogiro fly. They did see some movies of earlier flights.

Pitcairn asked Cierva if he would object if the Pitcairn organization made a helicopter out of the autogiro. Cierva merely shrugged and offered, "Go ahead if you can."

Pitcairn then revealed that he would be interested in obtaining manufacturing rights for the autogiro. Cierva assured the two that he had no reason to negotiate with anyone. The Spanish government financed all his experimental work. He further said that British, French, German, and Italian aircraft manufacturers had already approached him.

In the late summer of 1928 while Pitcairn's staff of designers was working on a highly advanced, smooth, stressed-skin biplane called the "Super Mailwing," designed to carry the U.S. mail, he returned to Europe and tried once more to negotiate with Cierva. This was the third time. He had tried once again after his 1925 visit. On this third visit, he had a flight in the Cierva C-8 autogiro. He was so impressed with the flight that he ordered one for study in America requesting, however, that it be powered by a Wright J5, 220 hp "Wirlwind" engine instead of

Original Pitcairn field in Bryn Athen, PA, a suburb of Philadelphia.   *(Pitcairn Photo)*

The site of the original Pitcairn Field as it is now. A modern low-cost housing development is now across the road.   *(Sacks Photo)*

The Pitcairn factory at Pitcairn field (now U.S. Navy Air Station) Willow Grove, PA. (Pitcairn Photo)

the 180 hp Viper which Cierva was using in the C-8 in 1925.

Pitcairn put himself and his staff in a position to concentrate their efforts on the autogiro development. He disposed of his airmail line. (Which later became Eastern Airlines.) Pitcairn's famous Mailwing was being used at that time on his own as well as twelve other airlines, and was to continue in service until 1936.

The C-8 arrived at Pitcairn Field, Willow Grove, Pennsylvania (now the Willow Grove Naval Air Station) in mid-December 1928. It was test flown on December 19 by Herbert Rawson, a British pilot.

On that day Paul Stanley, a very fine engineer, joined the Pitcairn organization. Paul became one of the foremost rotary-wing engineers.

The autogiro's performance on takeoff and climb was compared with the Mailwing's ability; with Pitcairn flying the autogiro. Pitcairn's Chief Pilot, Jim Ray, flew the Mailwing. The autogiro did such a fine job that Pitcairn completed negotiations with Cierva Autogiro Company (at that time in London) for manufacturing rights, forming the Autogiro Company of America. Pitcairn-Cierva Autogiro Company became the first licensee.

The first Pitcairn Autogiro almost became a Mailwing with a rotor installed. Pitcairn's staff

had learned from their evaluation of the C-8 that this was not the way to do it. The result was the PCA-1 (for Pitcairn-Cierva Autogiro 1) designed and built especially for the Autogiro requirements. It could not help, however, to show its fine Pitcairn lineage.

Because there was no mechanical rotor spin-up mechanism, the first autogiro required taxiing around the field, increasing the speed gradually to get the rotor up to takeoff rpm. Later a "box kite" tail that could have its horizontal surfaces tilted simultaneously to cause the propeller stream to be deflected up through the rotor was used. Although he used this system on his PCA-1, Pitcairn thought this system to be an "un-American" way to do things. He proceeded to design a mechanical rotor starter with the help of Machine Tool Design Company.

This unit was attached to the starter mounting pad on the Wright engine. A compressed air starter was used to crank the engine for starting. Credit is given to Jean Nichol, Machine Tool's designer, for the design of a twin-disc clutch and a rotor starter capable of carrying 15 to 20 horsepower to the blades. This was the maximum that Wright Aeronautical permitted to be run through the engine starting gear part of the engine. This turned the forty-two foot diameter PCA-1 rotor up to 80 or 90 rpm in 30 to 40 seconds requiring a very short ground run to

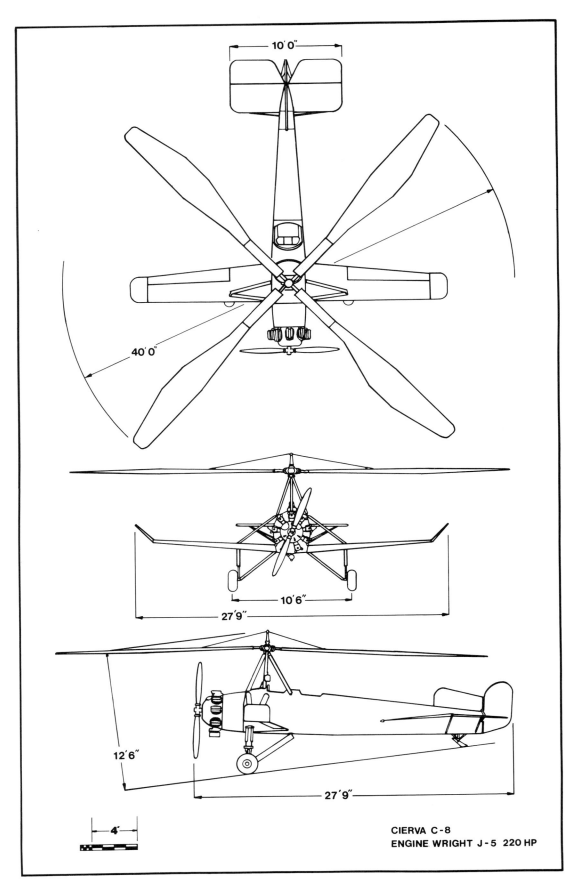

10' 0"

40' 0"

10' 6"

27' 9"

12' 6"

27' 9"

4'

CIERVA C-8
ENGINE WRIGHT J-5 220 HP

16

accelerate the rotor to 120 to 130 rpm necessary for takeoff. Without a torque compensating device, such as a helicopter tail rotor, the autogiro could not leave the ground while the rotor was powered.

Kellett, another licensee joined Pitcairn-Cierva's Autogiro Company of America. Next a successful manufacturer of fixed-wing aircraft, Buhl Aircraft of Marysville, Michigan. Their designer, Andre' Dormoy adapted a Pitcairn-style rotor and fixed wing arrangement to a pusher autogiro which was successfully flown on December 15, 1931. The test pilot was Buhl's Jimmy Johnson. Buhl never went further than this first model and did not obtain an approved type certificate.

Pitcairn went on with improvements to the PCA-1 and redesigned it to become the PCA-2. This was the first autogiro to obtain an Approved Type Certificate from the Department of Commerce (later CAA and now FAA).

Pitcairn's original factory was in Bryn Athyn, Pennsylvania. Their first fixed wing airplane was the "Fleetwing" a five-place open cockpit biplane unusual in that it had three cockpits in tandem. The forward carried two, the next, two and the rear cockpit was for the pilot. This craft was built to carry sightseeing passengers at the Philadelphia-hosted Sesqui-Centennial exposition in 1926.

Another airplane was being built by Pitcairn at the same time to race in two classes at the 1926 National Air Races being held at the Sesqui-Centennial. It was first called the "Fleet Arrow," but was later changed to the 'Sesqui-Wing" in honor of the Sesqui-Centennial exposition being held in 1926. The "Sesqui-Wing" surpassed all by winning both races. It was a sleek three-place open cockpit biplane. It was to race in the OX-5 engine class and, by employing a quick-change engine pod and a special crew, in the C-6 engine class.

The Pitcairn Fleet Arrow logo.

The next project was the "Orowing," a three-place OX-5 powered open biplane. It was named Orowing because the wings and tail of the Curtiss "Oriol" were mounted on a Pitcairn-built welded steel tube fuselage. This aircraft was intended to replace the famous World War I Curtiss JN-4 (Jenny) which was being sold surplus to barnstorming pilots.

Pitcairn's famous Mailwing came along next, built first as the model PA-4, a three-place open-cockpit biplane called "Fleetwing 2." Only five were built, most had OX-5 engines, but one had a 125 hp Kinner B-5 engine and one had a 110 hp Warner engine.

The style was redesigned slightly with a Wright Wirlwind J5, 220 hp plant and the model was the PA-5 Mailwing.

It was built for use on Pitcairn's Newark, New Jersey to Miami, Florida airmail line. Mailwings were also bought and used by fourteen other airmail operators; quite a tribute to this airplane.

The Mailwing was constantly improved through the PA-6, PA-7 and the PA-8. The design of a Super-Mailwing using smooth, stressed-skin design and having the best lift-to-drag ratio of any airplane ever tested at New York University was under way in the late summer of 1928.

The mail line was sold at the end of 1928 to permit the staff to spend more time on the autogiro project. Fixed-wing production was suspended in about 1931 and the PA-7 production line and spares were sold "as is." About seven sets of completed airplane parts were ready for assembly and most went to local aviators for sport and business use.

Autogiros designs went on, the next called PAA-1, which was said to be a "scaled-down PCA-2" with 125 horsepower. Most of these were modified to PA-20 with a larger rotor or PA-24 with a larger rotor and a 160 horsepower Kinner engine. An improved design was the PA-18, still a two-place open craft; smooth fuselage contours replaced the angular PA-20, PA-24 lines.

The need for a plush cabin autogiro was felt about 1931. Larsen told Pitcairn that there was not an engineer on the staff who had sufficient experience with cabin planes design. When asked who he would recommend, Larsen suggested Bob Noorduyn who was Bellanca's designer. Bellanca built the foremost cabin planes of the time. Noorduyn had also worked with Fokker, Sopwith and Whitworth. These were all prominent aircraft companies of the twenties.

In 1929 Pitcairn contracted for the only autogiro to be built outside his plant other than the original Cierva C-8 which he bought in 1928. The Spaniard who had given him the letter of introduction to Cierva, Heraclio Alfaro, proposed a two-place open cockpit 110 horsepower type. The contract was entered into in the summer of 1929. It was flown first on July 18, 1930, and was wrecked on the way to the Cleveland Air Races August 21, 1930. Although having several new and unusual features, Pitcairn did not see enough promise to go on with it. It was not rebuilt after the accident.

Alfaro had tried to get the position of Chief Engineer with the Pitcairn organization. When this relationship never did materialize, he negotiated to build his autogiro for Pitcairn.

Later a fourth licensee, Steere Engineering Company of White Plains, New York, was signed up. They had no previous experience in aircraft manufacture. When Alfaro did not get the job as Chief Engineer with Pitcairn, he went to work with Steere in that capacity. Steere bought a Pitcairn PAA-1 Autogiro, but they never developed a product of their own.

In December of 1930, Pitcairn announced that commercial autogiro production had begun. The machine that was designed for production was the three-place open cockpit PCA-2. The power was supplied by a Wright J6, seven cylinder 225 hp package. Before developments had gone very far, the engine was changed to a nine cylinder Wright of the J6 series. This one developed 300 hp. Some other refinements to the design took place.

Advertising brochures boasted a speed of "well over 100 mph." Landing speed was given as zero. Takeoff distance was described as a short run. Actually the distance necessary to lift off the ground at full gross weight depended, as usual, on air density and the wind velocity. Normally at sea level with no wind, the run was about two hundred feet. The rotor, it must be remembered, was not powered but turned by autorotation even during takeoff. A clutch was provided to bring the rotor up to a speed of 110/120 rpm, but it had to be disconnected before takeoff because there was no way to offset the rotor torque that would be present with a driven rotor. A rotor brake was provided to stop the rotor once the autogiro was on the ground.

The PCA-2 could be slowed to about 20 mph in the air while still holding altitude and under adequate control. Descents could be made safely at zero airspeed; it did, however, require a special skill to expertly land the craft after a zero airspeed descent. The nose must be dropped at precisely the right time to attain the airspeed necessary for elevator control in landing. There was no control in the rotor.

Two cockpits were installed, the pilot occupied the rear and two passengers could be carried in the front. A very small baggage compartment was located behind the pilot and was accessible from outside the fuselage.

The pylon which supported the rotor was refined from a four-legged structure to one having three legs. One leg extended forward and the other two ran aft to the outer edges of the forward side of the rear cockpit.

A group of Pitcairn aviation pilots. Left to right: Jim Falkner, Amberse Banks, Jim Ray, and Ben Falkner in front of a Pitcairn PA-5 "Mailwing."
(Pitcairn Photo)

18

Pitcairn PCA-1

Pitcairn PCA1-A showing boxtail for aerodynamic rotor spinup, before mechanical starter.   *(Pitcairn Photo)*

The PCA-1 could be recognized by its four-legged pylon. Earlier it was equipped with a box-like tail. The tail could be set nearly vertical so that the propeller stream would pass up through the rotor blades and bring them nearly up to takeoff speed. It also had an elaborate set of flying and landing wires on the wings. When the box kite tail was removed later, the vertical fin was carried all the way up to the cockpit behind the pilot's headrest. The fuselage was made from aluminum alloy tubing by the Hall Aircraft Company of Buffalo. The covering was fabric over a heavily faired superstructure. The construction of the box tail is not a matter of record but it is assumed to be aluminum alloy. It was definitely fabric covered. Wings were made with wood spars and ribs with fabric covering.

The engine was a geared Wright R-760 "Whirlwind" which developed 240 hp at 2,000 engine rpm. A novel magnesium three-bladed ground adjustable propeller 10 feet in diameter was installed. Rotor blades for this model were made by Cierva in England. They were covered with a very thin mahogany plywood with a natural wood finish.

The design nearly became a modified Mailwing with an autogiro rotor added. Instead, all components were designed and built to fill autogiro requirements. Cierva's autogiros had been airplanes modified to install his rotor systems. Too much penalty in weight and other compromises were found when Pitcairn evaluated the C-8 so that the decision was immediately made to design the complete autogiro.

It had been found in tests with the C-8 that the machine lacked directional stability. It was decided that it was caused by the large mass of the rotor high above the c.g. of the autogiro. Turned-up wing tips were soon added to the C-8 to help correct this, and they were to be characteristic and symbolic of the autogiro for some years.

To make the craft stable on the ground, a landing gear tread of twelve feet was used. The main elements of the PCA-1 landing gear were streamlined heat treated steel tubes welded into "vee" assemblies to carry the axles and "N" assemblies to carry the axle loads to the fuselage. The "N" assemblies were braced to each other and to the lower side of the fixed wing with alloy steel streamlined rods. The same type of tie rods continued the landing gear structure from the top of the wing to the fuselage. The welded "vee" assemblies were hinged to the lower end of the "N" struts and connected the lower end of the hydraulic shock struts. The upper end of the shock strut was connected to the bottom side of the wing.

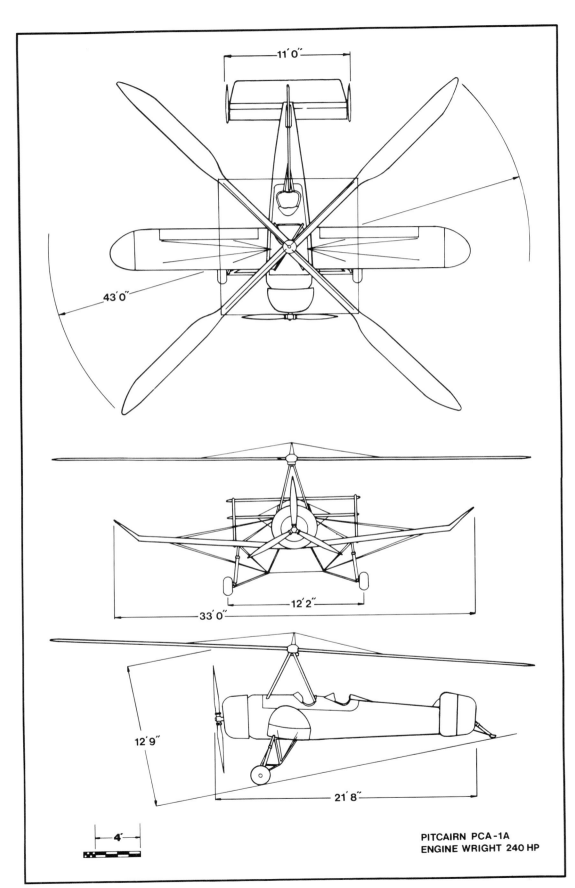

11′ 0″

43′ 0″

12′ 2″

33′ 0″

12′ 9″

21′ 8″

4′

PITCAIRN PCA-1A
ENGINE WRIGHT 240 HP

20

Additional streamlined tie rods were attached to the fuselage with their outer ends to the front and rear wing spars to act as landing wires. An equal number were attached from the landing gear "N" struts to the lower side of the wing for flying wires.

The ailerons ran the full length of the wing panel except for approximately one foot at the inboard end used for a footwalk.

The paint scheme was yellow wings and horizontal tail. (The boxkite tail was all yellow when installed) with black fuselage and landing gear. The finish was Pitcairn's usual hand-rubbed finish. The rotor blades, as mentioned, were varnished natural mahogany. Missing was Pitcairn's logo; the arrow, in yellow (or gold) with the cabin-like device hung below it.

Three PCA-1s were built, but one was destroyed in a fire at the Bryn Athyn factory. Department of Commerce approval was not applied for.

Principal dimensions: rotor diameter, 43 feet; disc area, 1462 sq. ft.; wingspan, 32 ft. 6 in.; wing chord (average), 46 in.; height, 14 ft. 2 in.

The PCA-1 was redesigned into the PCA-2 with some minor changes. The appearance was generally the same. The main differences were

Various autogiros, left to right: Cierva C19-III, PCA-1, PCA2 (#1), Alfaro and Cierva C-8.   *(Pitcairn Photo)*

Pitcairn PCA-1B-originally a PCIA with a box-like tail. The horizontal surfaces were bi-plane type and when the stick was full back the propeller stream was directed up through the rotor for an aerodynamic start. Note many flying and landing wires on wings.

(Pitcairn Photo)

21

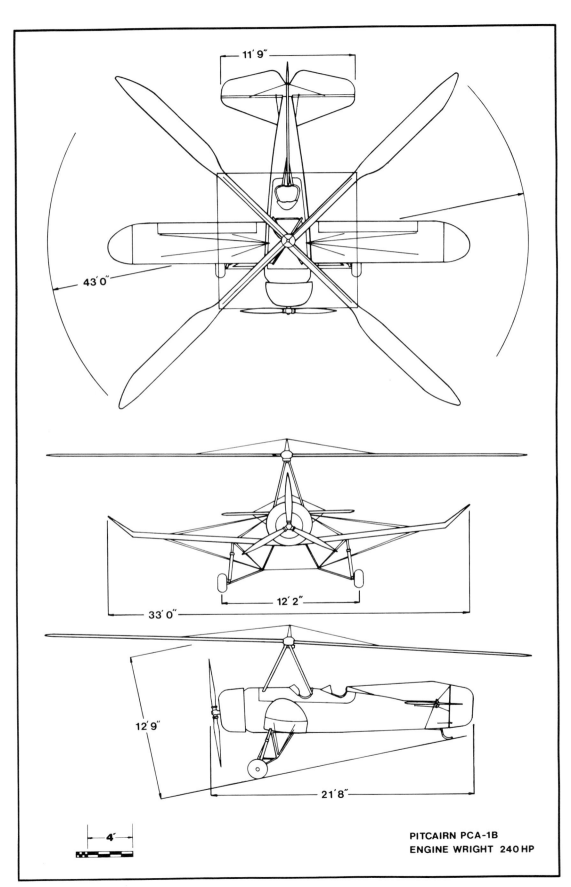

11′ 9″

43′ 0″

33′ 0″

12′ 2″

12′ 9″

21′ 8″

4′

PITCAIRN PCA-1B
ENGINE WRIGHT 240 HP

22

the change in the rotor pylon from four legs to three legs, elimination of the outboard flying and landing brace wires on the wings, and a slightly shorter landing gear.

The fuselage construction was welded steel tubes of varying diameters and wall thicknesses. The aluminum tubing fuselage on the PCA-1 was abandoned because of the difficulty of repair. The longerons on the PCA-2 were the familiar square shape that Pitcairn had used on all the Mailwing airplanes. The forward part of the fuselage around the cockpits was built with single tubes forming "vees" and "N's" to carry the loads from the landing gear, the wings and rotor pylon. Aft of the cockpit, the open bays formed by the longerons and cross members, were braced with two 3/16" diameter steel tubes welded diagonally from corner to corner of the bay and crossing each other in the center of the bay in the form of an "X." The engine mount was not removable from the fuselage, but was welded on as an integral part. Provisions were made in the engine mounting ring to install rubber bushings to absorb the engine vibrations. Deep fairing was built onto the fuselage to make the widest point as wide as the overall diameter of the engine. The frame for the tail surfaces was also welded steel tubing. The main beams of the tail surfaces where the hinges attached were of eliptical tubes. The airfoil section was added to these surfaces by building up the shape with small diameter steel tubes welded together and into the assembly. The entire tail group was bolted down to the fuselage and was wire braced. The horizontal stabilizer assembly could be adjusted in flight to trim the autogiro with varying loads.

The fixed wings had a total span of thirty feet and were built up in two panels bolted to the fuselage at a large dihedral angle. An M3 airfoil was selected. The left and right panels were built of spruce and birch, the main beams being built-up box assemblies.

The rotor blades were generally rectangular in plan form. The chord of the blade was of two widths; the one outboard being larger than the inboard. Transitional section of increasingly longer ribs faired the inner, narrow chord to the wider outer chord. The tip was curved with its thickness tapering into a rather sharp edge at the tip. Drain holes were provided at several places along the trailing edge of the blade to ventilate the inside to expel any moisture that was present as the result of condensation. These holes also prevented air pressure being built up from the centrifugal pumping caused by the rotation

of the blade. The outer chord width was 22 inches; the inboard 5¾ feet had a chord of only 14-25/32 inches, the transition required three feet from inner to outer. The main member was a round tube of 4130 steel, 2⅛ inches in diameter straightened to a close tolerance, heat treated and hand polished. Approximately fifty plywood ribs, an average of three inches apart, formed the airfoil. A Pitcairn #4 air foil was developed. It was a modification of the Goetingen 429. Ribs were routed from five-ply wood having alternate layers of mahogany and birch and were one quarter of an inch thick. Each rib had a stainless steel collar riveted onto one side, and these in turn were fastened to the steel spar. Some of the early blades had these collars soldered to the spar, but this was later changed to spot welding. The welding process was especially developed by Pitcairn engineers so that the maximum strength in the weld could be developed without reducing the strength of the spar tube in the process. The blade was covered to a point just aft of the spar tube with thin plywood that had been preformed to the leading edge shape. The trailing edge was formed into a stainless steel "vee" of thin sheet which was nailed to the ribs on earlier models. Later a steel tail was formed for each rib and the wood rib cut off blunt about three inches from the end of the rib. The stainless steel trailing edge was provided with slip joints so that one section of the trailing edge telescoped into the other if the blade flexed fore and aft. As the entire blade was finished in doped fabric, the slip joints were covered with small leather patches so as not to wear out the trailing edge fabric. The fabric was held down to the ribs by rib stitching in the same manner as an airplane wing.

Each blade was attached to the hub through a flapping hinge which permitted the blade to flap up and down in balancing the forces of lift and centrifugal tension. The result of the two forces caused the blade to assume a "coning angle" above the horizontal. This angle varied, depending on whether the blade was advancing into the air stream or retreating from it. Just outboard of this flapping hinge a vertical hinge was installed. This permitted the blade to lag back as the drag was higher going into the air stream and to move forward as the drag decreased while the blade traveled with the airstream. To somewhat control the "hunting" of the blade as it traveled around the circumference of its circle, the blades were connected together with a steel cable about eight feet from the center of rotation. To prevent heavy shock loads in the blades as

The tail group for the Pitcairn PCA-1A with the horizontal tail in the normal position. (Pitcairn Photo)

The tail group for the Pitcairn PCA1-A with the horizontal tail deflected as it would be to deflect the air through the rotor for aerodynamic rotor start. (Pitcairn Photo)

they did their leading and lagging, a hydraulic shock absorber which was actually a reworked hydraulic door closer was installed between the cable and the blade spar. At the hub, on either side of each vertical hinge pin, two rubber blocks were installed to take up the shock if the blades were put in motion with their hydraulic damper at the extreme end of its travel. To prevent the blades from dropping all the way down on their flapping hinge and striking the aircraft when they were at rest or slowing down. A "droop" cable was run from a small cone or tower mounted on top of the hub to a point just inboard of the lead-lag damper.

The hub itself was mounted on bearings which were in turn mounted on a stationary axle or mast. This mast was fitted into the tripod or "pylon" which attached to the fuselage and lifted the autogiro into the air when the rotor provided sufficient lift.

The landing gear was similar to the PCA-1. The main gear was originally fitted with 30x5 high pressure tires which were changed to "semi-balloon" 850x10 tires. The tread was widened to thirteen feet, six inches. The bracing arrangement was the same as the PCA-1. A long-travel oleo shock strut was used. As in the PCA-1, the tail landing gear was a full-swiveling tail skid with rubber cord shock absorber.

The PCA-2 employed a mechanical rotor starter to bring the rotor up to the necessary takeoff rpm. This was mounted on the pad normally used by the engine starter. This required another means of starting the engine. A "Heywood Products" air starter injected compressed air directly into the engine cylinder. Air forced the piston down and turned the propeller to start the engine. A small air compressor mounted on the accessory pad developed 500 psi air pressure which was stored in a small tank. When

released with a handle in the cockpit, air was delivered to the proper cylinder(s) in the firing order. Priming fuel, if used, was injected into the air line with a primer. No electrical system was installed. If position lights were desired, a dry "hot-shot" battery powered the lights. The battery was not rechargeable.

The fuel system consisted of two tanks. One 13-gallon tank just ahead of the passengers supplied fuel to the engine by gravity. Another 39-gallon tank was installed just below the cockpit floorline (actually under the passenger's seat). An engine-driven fuel pump kept the gravity tank full as long as fuel was available in the 39-gallon tank. All the while fuel was being delivered to the gravity tank a fuel pressure gauge in the cockpit showed fuel pressure. When the main tank fuel was exhausted, fuel pressure dropped to zero. The engine would continue to run because fuel was arriving from the gravity tank. The small tank had no fuel quantity gauge. It was necessary to constantly scan the pressure gauge because at the second the needle dropped to zero the upper tank was full for the last time. It was considered that a "safe" twenty minutes fuel remained with time to make a landing. The quantity gauge on the main tank was not a constant-reading type. It was necessary to pull a plunger out of the instrument panel and release it. This caused the fuel quantity to show on the quantity gauge.

The engine oil tank carried six and one half gallons and was mounted on the fire wall.

A conventional control stick rising from the floor operated the elevators and ailerons for pitch and roll control. Rudder pedals gave yaw control through a rudder at the rear of the fuselage. All controls were cable operated.

Just inboard of each rudder pedal was a similar pedal which operated the mechanical

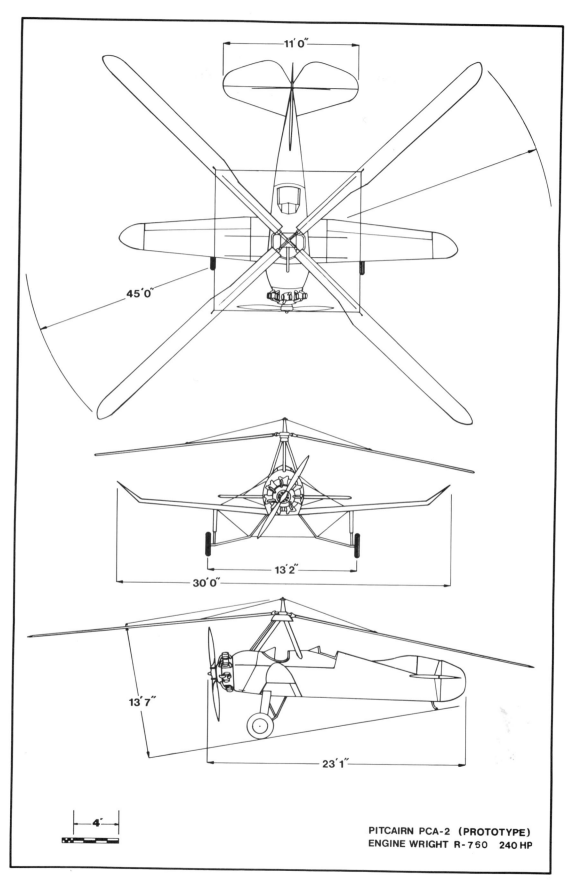

11′ 0″

45′ 0″

13′ 2″

30′ 0″

13′ 7″

23′ 1″

4′

PITCAIRN PCA-2 (PROTOTYPE)
ENGINE WRIGHT R-760 240 HP

Pitcairn PCA-2 accident at an air show in Philadelphia in 1932. The pilot had just demonstrated a "dead stick" landing to the crowd. He took off with the fuel shut off. Enough fuel was in the lines and carburetor to get the autogiro airborne. The pilot turned the fuel on when the engine stopped and stroked the wobble pump. The engine came back on at full throttle. rolling the autogiro onto its side.   (Pitcairn Photo)

Pitcairn PCA-2 taking off from a dock in New York City.   (Pitcairn Photo)

wheel brakes using a cable. It was necessary to move one's feet from the rudder pedals to the brake pedals when taxiing or taking off when brake or rudder control was needed. The Mailwing used the same system. It became critical on the Mailwing for the pilot to slide his feet to the proper pedal at exactly the right time on takeoff as the rudder became active and on the landing as it became useless. It was not as critical on the PCA-2 with its nearly-zero landing speed.

The PCA-2 came through the same factory, was groomed by the same fine craftsmen, and was designed by the same engineers as the Mailwing, so it had a family resemblance. But, as said earlier, it was learned from the experience at Pitcairn with the Cierva C-8 that the autogiro should not be a conventional airplane with rotor on top. It was built, like the Mailwing, to be flown by professional pilots. It proved to be a fine aircraft and saw service for many years with the Horizon Company, Fairchild Aircraft Company, Morgon Oil Company, Tri-State Airways, Champion Spark Plug Company, Standard Oil Company, Beech Nut, Standard Oil of Ohio, Detroit News, Pure Oil, Silverbrook Coal, as an advertising tool of Lee Tire Company, and others. The U.S. Marine Corps purchased a

PCA-2 designated the XOP-1 and gave it service tests in Nicaragua. They thought it had some attributes, however, fitted with military gear very little payload was available. No further orders were forthcoming.

Among the PCA-2's early accomplishments was a flight across the United States when this was still a feat for fixed wing aircraft, an early flight across the straits of Florida to Cuba, and after installation of a special auxiliary tank on across Central America. One PCA-2 was looped as an everyday attraction by an airshow. Using the PCA-2 as a camera platform several newspapers were able to bring back unusual news pictures, among them the pictures of the ocean liner Moro Castle burning off the east coast of New Jersey on a very foggy day. One PCA-2 was landed and taken off from the White House lawn by Jim Ray when Harold Pitcairn was presented with the Collier Trophy by President Herbert Hoover.

The other variations of the PCA-2, differing only in the engine that was installed, were produced but not in quantity. A PCA-3 mounted a Pratt and Whitney Wasp Jr. engine, delivering 300 hp. The PA-21 used a Wright R-975 plant with 450 hp. In all, about 24 of all of the PCA-2

PCA-2 Pitcairn Autogiro over New York City, 1930.   *(Aero Service/Pitcairn Photo)*

The author pulling the Pitcairn PCA-2
Autogiro up at the end of a crop dusting
run. When the dust hopper gate is shut,
the dust cloud under the autogiro will
magically drop back into the crop field
the autogiro has just left.
(Gus Pasquarella Photo)

Pitcairn PCA-2 crop duster with the
author in the cockpit. This was serial
number 13; The one with which Johny
Miller performed loops in the "American Air Aces" show in 1933.
(Photo by Charles Gilfillan)

Pitcairn PCA-2 treating crops with
insecticide dust. The author is the
pilot. (Gus Pasquarella Photo)

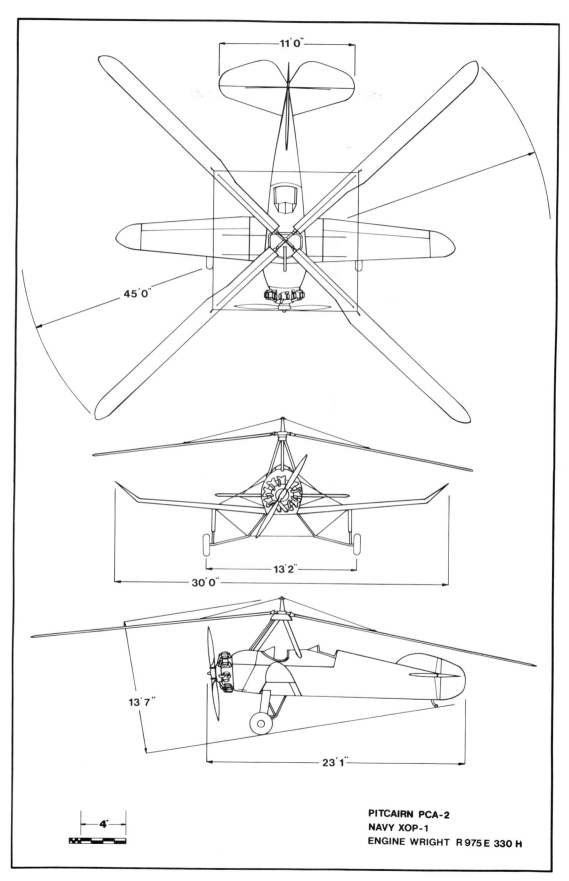

11'0"

45'0"

13'2"

30'0"

13'7"

23'1"

4'

PITCAIRN PCA-2
NAVY XOP-1
ENGINE WRIGHT R 975 E 330 H

The author "on the deck" of his Pitcairn PCA-2 dusting autogiro.
(Gus Pasquarella Photo)

variations were completed. None is known to be still flying. The one formerly owned by the Detroit News is in the Ford Museum in Detroit. Another formerly owned by the Department of Agriculture as a PCA-2 was modified in 1946 to a PA-21 and did some crop spraying in New England. It gradually deteriorated and was last heard from in the hands of a gentleman in Seattle, Washington who had hopes of restoring it.

Several pilots looped the autogiro. John Miller performed loops every day with the American Air Aces Show in the mid-thirties. Charlie Otto who flew advertising banners for Lee Tire and Rubber Company looped his PCA-2 in the thirties.

A report was found in the Pitcairn archives and says a pilot, D. W. Dean, looped a PCA-2 at the Pitcairn factory on October 13, 1931.

The U.S. Marine Corps bought three PCA-2s designated XOP-1s, one of which was used in Nicaragua with the Marine Corps. The XOP-1 did not receive a fair test, however, because the pilot assigned to the flying had never flown a rotating-wing aircraft before.

The civilian paint schemes varied with the desires of the buyers. Pitcairn's demonstrator

Pitcairn PCA-2 Autogiro belonging to Amelia Earhart.
(Pitcairn Photo)

(NR 760W) was nearly all black in a hand-rubbed finish. A patch of light green in sort of a tear drop shape ran down each side of the fuselage. The black and green were separated with a narrow ivory stripe. The rotor blades were ivory with a narrow green strip span-wise, at the tip it divided into two stripes, one running to the leading edge, and one running to the trailing edge framing a light green tip. All numbering and lettering was light green.

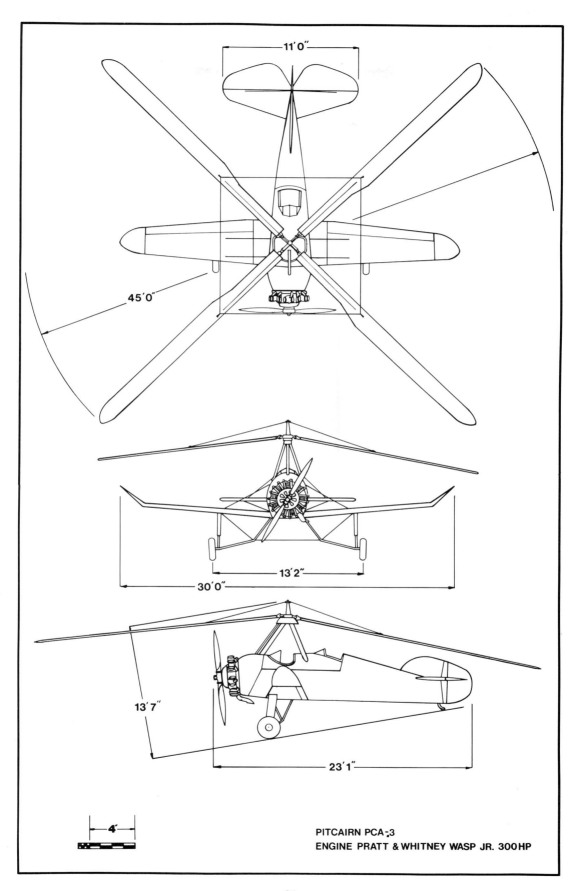

11' 0"

45' 0"

30' 0"

13' 2"

13' 7"

23' 1"

4'

PITCAIRN PCA-3
ENGINE PRATT & WHITNEY WASP JR. 300HP

Pitcairn PCA-2 (PCA-3) rotor blade frome, 22" chord aproximately 22 ft. long.   *(Pitcairn Photo)*

Champion PCA-2 Autogiro, originally manufactured in 1931 for the Champion Spark Plug Company. The author completed the restoration to flying condition in 1985 for Stephen Pitcairn.   *(Pitcairn Photo)*

Pitcairn Navy XOP-Autogiros. X (Experimental)
O (Observation) P (Pitcairn) 1 first model.
(Pitcairn Photo)

Left side of Navy XOP-1 engine compartment. (Pitcairn
PCA- 2) (National Archives Photo)

Navy XOP-1

(National Archives)

The Collier Trophy presentation to Harold F. Pitcairn. Mr. Pitcairn is shaking hands with President Hoover. Orville Wright is 4th from left with dark suit, Jim Ray is in the white suit, 6th from left, Agnew Larsen is to Jim's left.　　　　　*(Pitcairn Photo)*

Pitcairn PCA-2 taking off from the street in Washington, D.C., Jim Ray is the pilot.
(Pitcairn Photo)

Pitcairn PCA-2 and PCA-3

Pitcairn PCA-2 No. 13 owned and flown by John Miller. He looped this autogiro everyday with an air show in the 30's.

(John Underwood Photo)

"CAA AIRCRAFT LISTING"
PITCAIRN PCA-2 and PA-21, 3 POLAg,
ATC 410

(Models PCA-2 and PA-21 identical except engine installation)

Engine	Wright R-975 330 hp (Model PCA-2)
	Wright R-975E-2 420 hp (Model PA-21)
Fuel	52 gals. (One 39 gal. tank under passenger seat and one 13 gal. tank rear of firewall)
Oil	6½ gals.
No. pass.	2
Baggage	36 lbs.
Standard weight	3000 lbs.
Spec. basis	Approved Type Certificate No. 410
Serial Nos.	B-5 and up mfrd. prior to 9-30-39 eligible. Approval expired as of that date.

Class I equipment: Starter (Heywood); Propeller—adj. metal; Low pressure tires; Clevel and A-3319 shock absorber struts.

Class III equipent:

Flares 45 lbs.; Aux. 20 gal. fuel tank 14 lbs.; Bendix R-119-04d shock absorber struts, no change in weight; Replacement or repair of rotor blades to include metal trailing edge section and wooden stringer in leading edge running entire length of blade, net increase 16 lbs. (4 lbs. per blade).

"CAA AIRCRAFT LISTING"
PITCAIRN PCA-3, 3 POLAg,
ATC 446

Engine	P & W Wasp Jr. 300 hp
Propeller	Adj. metal (See NOTE 1)
Fuel	52 gals.
Oil	6 gals.
No. pass.	2

**AUTOGIRO COMPANY
OF AMERICA**

LOOPING OF PCA-2 AUTOGIRO

On October 13, 1931, at approximately 2 P.M., Mr. D. W. Dean looped the PCA-2 Autogiro No. B-15 twice. He says that on his first loop he thought he pulled the stick back too sharply, causing it to fall out of the last part of the maneuver, while the second one was a clean, normal loop. He said that the Autogiro felt no different from an airplane, while he was going through these loops. Some observers from the ground apparently disagree, saying that they could observe very little difference in the two loops, as at the completion of each there seemed to be a tendency to fall out to the right; while others agree that the second loop was the best.

Mr. Dean's speed as he went into each loop was 120 M.P.H. He did not obtain his rotor R.P.M. during the loop, but in a tight turn he accelerated the rotor to 180 R.P.M.

The looping of an Autogiro, which has been considered as theoratically possible as long as the loop was clean, has now been practically demonstrated.

Paul H. Stanley.
Paul H. Stanley

Several pilots looped the autogiro. John Miller performed loops every day with the American Air Aces Show in the mid thirties. Charlie Otto who flew advertising banners for Lee Tire and Rubber Company looped his PCA-2 in the thirties.

A report was found in the Pitcairn archives and says a pilot, D. W. Dean, looped a PCA-2 at the Pitcairn factory on October 13, 1931.   *(Pitcairn Photo)*

Pitcairn PCA-2 owned by the Detroit News. Last heard of it was in the Ford Museum in Dearborn, Michigan.   *(Pitcairn Photo)*

Baggage   15 lbs. (Pay load includes 3
                 parachutes 20 lbs. each)
Standard weight 3063 lbs.
Spec. basis   Approved Type Certificate
                 No. 446
Serial Nos.   E-43 and up mfrd. prior to 9-
                 30-39 eligible. Approval ex-
                 pired as of that date.

Class III equipment: Extra 20 gal. fuel tank 14
lbs., Bendix R-119-04D shock struts; Flares 45
lbs.
NOTE 1. Serial No. E-45 eligible with controllable metal propeller, 42 lbs. net increase incl. 12
lbs. of ballast.

The preceeding are the equivalent of the FAA
"Spec. Data Sheets." The Spec. Data Sheets are
more comprehensive. The letters 3 POLAg in
each case mean 3 Place Open Land Autogiro.
ATC 410 was granted April 2, 1931. ATC 446
was granted August 5, 1931.

Specifications

	PCA-2	PCA-3
Gross Weight	3000 lb.	3063 lb.
E. Wt.	2093 lb.	
Useful load	907 lb.	915 lb.
Max speed	118 mph	120 mph
Cruise speed	98 mph	100 mph
Landing speed	20–24 mph	28–30 mph
Range	290 mi.	—

Pitcairn PAA-1 and PAA-2

Pitcairn PAA1. Note: Tailskid, three strut rotor pylon (the other from the rotor.) Going forward is rotor spinup shaft); landing gear shock strut upper end goes to an outrigger assembly ahead of the fixed wing leading edge. (Pitcairn Photo)

In 1930 when Pitcairn began production on the PCA-2 he was chided as well as applauded for the machine's performance. The inference was that, although the autogiro was a seeming success, it was large and expensive and required the services of a professional pilot.

This annoyed Pitcairn and he accepted the challenge to produce a light autogiro which would be safe for the novice to fly.

The product was an aircraft which has been referred to as a scaled model of the PCA-2. To the critical eye it did not closely resemble the PCA-2. The gross weight and the engine power were approximately one half of the PCA-2 figures.

The first attempt at a light autogiro was a PAA-2 with a 120 hp in-line Martin Chevrolet air-cooled engine. This craft lacked performance and a Kinner B5 of 125 hp was substituted. This model became a PAA-1.

The Martin engine delivered 120 hp at 2100 rpm while the Kinner gave 125 hp with only 1925 rpm, permitting the use of an eight-foot diameter propeller instead of the seven foot, nine inch prop that the Martin could swing. This

gave the Kinner powered combination more acceleration which was the most important action for an autogiro.

The construction of the fuselage was the same as the PCA-2, except of course smaller. It presented a rather slab-sided appearance because it was so lightly faired to save weight. The turtle deck from the cockpit to the tail was the only part that was noticeably faired. The lower engine cowl which originally housed the in-line Martin engine angled up to meet the five-cylinder radial Kinner.

The wing, as on the PCA-2, was made with box spars and built up ribs. Drag and anti-drag wires braced the wing internally. Light plywood covered the top and bottom leading edge back to the spar. The airfoil was a Goetingen 429 "modified." The wing was wire-braced to the fuselage and to the landing gear. The tail group originally resembled a scale model of the PCA-2, but additional dorsal and ventral fins had to be added to achieve satisfactory directional stability. These were installed above and below the horizontal stabilizer.

There is some confusion why the PAA-2

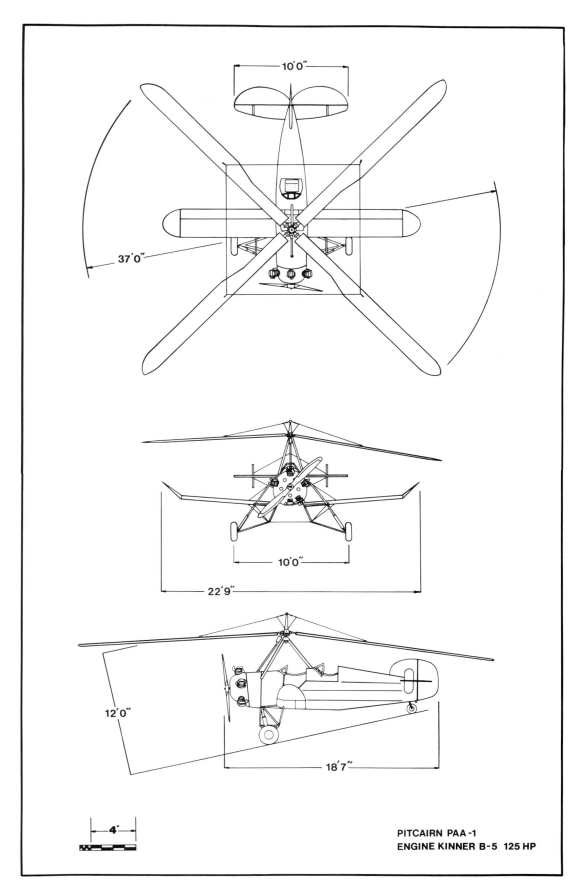

10'0"

37'0"

10'0"

22'9"

12'0"

18'7"

4'

PITCAIRN PAA-1
ENGINE KINNER B-5 125 HP

A PAA-1 with tailwheel, offered as a factory option. Built for the private owner, it was somewhat shy on performance with its 125 hp. engine, but it could operate from places no fixed wing airplane could. *(Pitcairn Photo)*

came before the PAA-1. Pitcairn's three-view drawing of the PAA-2 is dated a few days ahead of the PAA-2 drawing. Larsen, Pitcairn's Chief Engineer, said that the PAA-2 was tried and lacked performance.

The landing gear had the characteristic wide tread. The long oleo struts were attached at their upper ends to a cabane structure that in turn attached to the fuselage and the front wing spar. A tail skid, using a rubber cord shock absorber was installed similarly to the PCA-2. Mechanical brakes, controlled by pedals in the cockpit, aided in ground handling. A small nose wheel could be added to protect the propeller in case of a nose-up which could be caused by a rebounding of the tail shock absorber.

The rotor system had been referred to as a scaled-down model of the PCA-2 rotor. The same system of support and interblade cables, dampers and hinges were used. The rotor blade spar tubes were the same hand-polished, hand-straightened 4130 heat-treated steel, but the tubes were of a smaller diameter.

The Kinner engine was started with the same kind of compressed air starter as was used to start the Wright Whirlwind on the PCA-2. The propeller installation was optional: wood, fixed-

pitch aluminum or ground-adjustable aluminum.

The pilot flew from the rear cockpit and all the instruments necessary to operate the autogiro were in the rear cockpit except the rotor tachometer which was mounted on the bottom of the rotor mast so it could be seen from either cockpit. Some autogiros had air speed indicators and altimeters in the front cockpit also. Enclosures were installed over the rear cockpit on a few PAA-1s. They may have been considered PA-24s.

There was no standard color, but black was found on most of the autogiros.

After the PAA-1s were put into use they, too, were found to lack takeoff performance. Some PAA-1s were designated PA-20, most of both models were modified to PA-24s. This modification consisted of adding an R-5 Kinner engine of 160 hp in place of the B-5 and the rotor diameter was increased from 37 to 40 feet.

To keep the PAA-1 in longitudinal trim with or without a passenger in the front, a 16-pound lead slug was installed just ahead of the tail post without a passenger, and it was removed and installed in a pocket alongside the front seat (on the center of gravity) when the front seat was occupied.

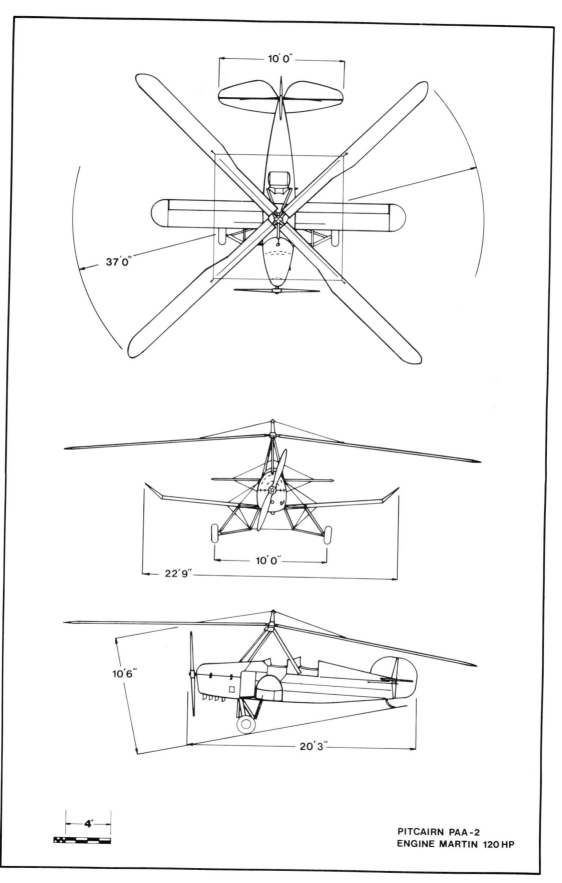

10' 0"

37' 0"

22' 9"

10' 0"

10' 6"

20' 3"

4'

PITCAIRN PAA-2
ENGINE MARTIN 120 HP

Pitcairn PAA-2 with Martin-Chevrolet 120 hp air-cooled in-line engine. Note "Training Wheel," no vertical auxiliary surfaces yet.
(Pitcairn Photo)

Pitcairn PAA-2. Note: Nose "training" wheel; no auxiliary vertical fins on tail; three strut pylon with two struts aft and one forward engine is Martin-Chevrolet in line 4 cylinder air-cooled—120 hp.
(Pitcairn Photo)

Pitcairn PA-20 (PAA-1)

Pitcairn PAA-1 (PA-20) at rear, then PCA-2 and what appears to be four PAA-1 autogiros. (Pitcairn Photo)

"CAA AIRCRAFT LISTING"
PITCAIRN PA-20 (or PAA-1), 2 POLAg,
ATC 433

Engine	Kinner B-5 125 hp
Fuel	27 gals.
Oil	3½ gals.
No. pass.	1
Baggage	44 lbs. (Includes 2 parachutes 20 lbs. each or seat cushions, used when parachutes are not worn, 12 lbs. each)
Standard weight	1800 lbs.
Spec. basis	Approved Type Certificate No. 433
Serial Nos.	19, 22 and up mfrd. prior to 9-30-39 eligible. Approval expired as of that date.

Class I equipment: Lead ballast 16 lbs.; Auxiliary fins 4 lbs.; Battery 10 lbs.; Starter 27 lbs.; Propeller adj. metal.

Class III equipment: Propeller fixed metal, net increase 20 lbs.; Safety wheel installation 12 lbs.; Three 1-Min. flares 9 lbs.; 10x3 tail wheel, no change in weight as 5 lbs. ballast must be removed from rear of fuselage for this installation.

NOTE 1. Serial Nos. 19, 32 to 41, incl., 52 to 56, incl., and 72 have manufacturer's name-plates with the model designation PAA-1. Certificates should be issued accordingly as manufacturer desires these autogiros to remain as PAA-1.

Specifications

Gross weight	1770 lbs.
Empty weight	1198 lbs.
Useful load	572 lbs.
Top speed	93 mph
Cruise speed	79 mph
Landing speed	*0 to 15 mph

*Some specs show "0" landing speed and others "20–25"

These are factory-released figures in a letter to *Aviation* magazine dated April 14, 1933. The gross weight, above, does not agree with the CAA Aircraft Listing which shows a gross of 1800 lbs. The release included the following: gravity fuel system, dual controls, "motor" starter, primer, metal propeller, semi-low pressure tires, tail wheel, fire extinguisher, navigation lights, leather upholstery, safety glass windshields, hand-rubbed glossy finish. F.O.B. Willow Grove $4940. The term was usually "FAF" Flyaway Factory.

Pitcairn PA-18

A rare, probably one-of-a-kind, PA-18 with a "coupe top," owned by Gilbert Flying Service of Valley Stream, New York.

(Pitcairn Photo)

The PA-18 and PAA-1 (PA-20) looked very much alike. It was difficult in fact, unless someone was very familiar with each, to recognize the differences. A note to *Aviation* from Ed Rice, the Director of Public Information of the Pitcairn organization, says the PA-20 was built as a "companion model" to the PA-18. A decision was made to discontinue manufacture of the PA-20 about April 14, 1933 because of the similarity to the PA-18.

The PA-18 was somewhat more pleasing in appearance. A well-rounded fuselage made the Kinner B-5 engine look more like it belonged there than it did on the PA-20.

Construction of the fuselage was the same as all preceding Pitcairn Autogiros. An assortment of steel tube diameters and wall thicknesses were expertly gas welded together. The sides and bottom of the fuselage were rounded out with wood fairing strips.

The tail group was nearly identical to the PAA-1. The only noticeable difference was the shape of the auxiliary vertical fins.

The wing was identical in construction details to the PAA-1, the span was decreased and the chord increased. The ailerons stopped short on the fuselage end to permit the walkway to extend to the trailing edge.

The main landing gear was a scaled-down PCA-2 landing gear. The tail gear was a small wheel with a rubber chord shock absorber.

A Kinner R-5, 160 hp engine turned a fixed-pitch Curtiss-Reed metal propeller eight feet, four inches in diameter. A ground adjustable propeller was optional at an increase of five pounds. A "coupe top" was also optional.

The rotor was identical to the PAA-1 (PA-20, PA-24) except that it was 40 feet in diameter. The rotor pylon was simplified to one fore and one aft member with wire bracing from the top of the pylon to the upper longerons.

The factory specifications from a brochure printed in 1932 again differ slightly from the CAA "listing":

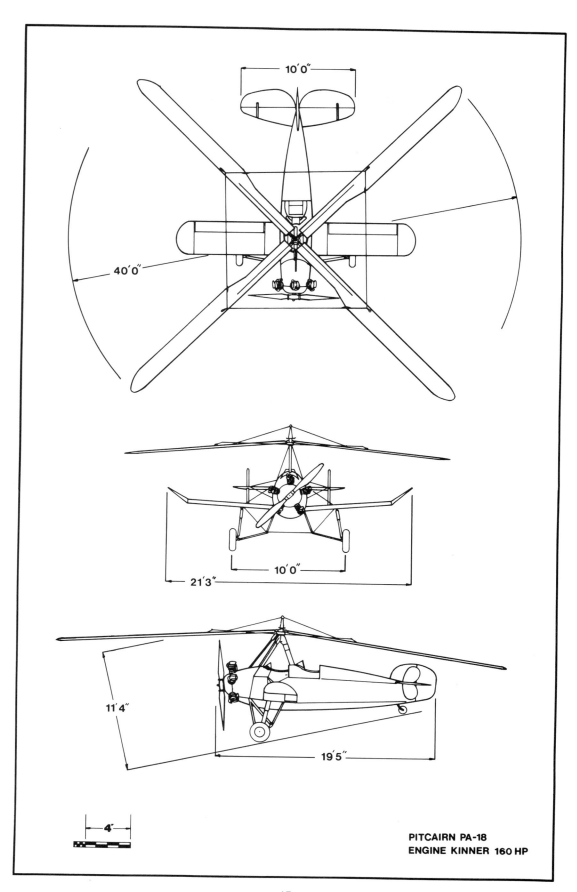

10′0″

40′0″

10′0″

21′3″

11′4″

19′5″

4′

PITCAIRN PA-18
ENGINE KINNER 160 HP

"CAA AIRCRAFT LISTING"
PITCAIRN PA-18, 2 PO-CLAg,
ATC 478

Engine	Kinner R-5 160 hp.
Fuel	30 gals.
Oil	3½ gals.
No. pass.	1
Baggage	10 lbs.
Standard wt.	1950 lbs.
Spec. Basis	Approved Type Cert. No. 478
Serial Nos.	G-62 and up mfrd. prior to 9-30-39 eligible. Approval expired as of that date.

Class I equipment: Fixed metal propeller; Dual controls; Seat cushions 9 lbs.; Battery 10 lbs.; Heywood starter 32 lbs.; 10 lbs. ballast in tail. Class III equipment: Safety wheel installation 12 lbs.; Adj. metal propeller, 5 lbs. net increase; Coupe top 3 lbs. net increase.

Specifications

Gross weight	1900 lbs.
Empty weight	1310 lbs.
Useful load	590 lbs.
Fuel capacity	30 gal.
Oil capacity	4 gal.

Pitcairn PA-18 built about 1931 for the sportsman and private user. About 19 of these were built and sold. Seven or eight of these were recalled during WWII and rebuilt as PA-39. All but one of them were lost when their transport was sunk. Note auxiliary nose "training" wheel. (Pitcairn Photo)

Pitcairn PA-18 at Wings Field near Philadelphia. Pilot Paul "Skip" Lukens, owner, and passenger Ann Strawbridge of the department store family. (Pitcairn Photo)

Pitcairn PA-18

(Pitcairn Photo)

Pitcairn PA-18 demonstrating "dead stick" landing.

(Pitcairn Photo)

Left to right. Pitcairn PA-36 (2) AC35, PA-22 and PA-18 inside the Pitcairn Factory, now by Tinius-Olsen Testing Company in Horsham (Willow Grove) PA. (Pitcairn Photo)

James G. Ray, Pitcairn's chief pilot. Beside a PA-18 autogiro. (Pitcairn Photo)

The fate of some PA-18s caused by applying power suddenly when flying too slow for aileron control. (Howard Levy Photo)

A Pitcairn PA-18 at a Detroit Aircraft show in the thirties.　　　　　　　　*(Pitcairn Photo)*

Italian pilot, Tito Falconi and movie actress Jean Harlow of the thirties, in front of a Pitcairn PA-18.　　*(John Underwood Photo)*

Pitcairn PA-24

Pitcairn PA-20 owned by Earle Eckel, modified with an enclosure over the rear cockpit. This is not considered a PA-24, which had both cock-pits covered.
(Pitcairn Photo)

"CAA AIRCRAFT LISTING"
PITCAIRN PA-24, 2 POLAg,
ATC 507

Engine	Kinner B-5 160 hp
Fuel	27 gals. (One in fuselage)
Oil	3½ gals.
No. pass.	1
Baggage	13 lbs.
Standard weight	1800 lbs.
Spec. basis	Approved Type Certificate No. 507
Serial Nos.	57 to 61 eligible. (See NOTE 1)

Class I equipment: Starter (Heywood) 32 lbs.; Ballast 16 lbs.; Auxiliary fins 4 lbs.; Safety wheel 12 lbs.; Propeller adj. metal.
NOTE 1. Serial Nos. 19, 32 to 41, incl., 52 to 56, incl., and 72 (formerly model PAA-1 or PA-20) eligible for conversion to this Model provided Curtiss 55511-48 propeller is used with diameter of 8 ft. and repitched to 57 in.

Specifications

Gross weight	1750 lbs.
Empty weight	1178 lbs.
Useful load	572 lbs.
Top speed	90 mph
Cruise	75 mph
Landing speed	20–25 mph
Rate of climb (first minute)	550 fpm
Service ceiling	10,000 ft.
Selling price	$7,650.00

A total of about twenty-five autogiros consisting of models PAA-1, PA-24, PA-20 were built. A memo from W. C. Clayton of Pitcairn Engineering Department announces the model differences:

"s/n s F-18 to F-21, F-32 to F-41, F-52 to F-56 and F-72 are PAA-1s and are not to be changed. s/n s F-57 to F-61 are PA-20s. Any PA-20 or PAA-1 could be changed to a PA-24 by installing a Kinner B-5 engine."

The memo is dated May 9, 1933. Performance is not given. Approved Type Certificate 478 was granted April 7, 1932. Metal prop was standard electrical or air starter, fire extinguisher, navigation lights and dual controls were optional.

Pitcairn PA-19

Pitcairn PCA-2, PA-19, Kellet K-3, PAA-1 and PA-18 autogiros at Pitcairn Field.

(Pitcairn Photo)

Late in 1932, the Pitcairn Autogiro Company announced that after extensive flight tests on an experimental model they were ready to produce a four-place cabin autogiro designated the PA-19. This design was the work and responsibility of Robert B. C. Noorduyn who had recently joined the Pitcairn organization as Executive Engineer. Noorduyn had previously held the position of Vice President with Bellanca. The announcement stated that several new features were included in the design of this craft. The chief new feature was the "tilt-adjusting rotor." This meant that the pilot could select an optimum setting for the angle of the rotor hub axis. The control of this axis was through the use of a crank in the ceiling of the autogiro like an adjustable stabilizer or trim tab control found in the cabin ceiling of many aircraft today. Five full turns of the crank would adjust the rotor axis from one end of the travel to the other. Changing the angle in this way permitted the aircraft to accommodate a greater center of gravity range. Other features were the cantilever arrangement of the wings, tail surfaces and landing gear. The net result of these features in design combined both good autogiro characteristics with stability and control expected of well-designed fixed-wing aircraft of the day. The main criteria considered according to the manufacturer were strength, reliability, ease of maintenance, comfort and appearance.

The fuselage frame was constructed of welded steel tubing. Particular attention was paid to the designing of the structure to avoid placing of structural members across the area covered by windows or pilot's windshield. The design and shape of the fuselage was chosen to give maximum visibility from the pilot's position and to afford most comfort to the passengers. The engine was kept as low as possible in order to improve the visibility for the pilot. The fuselage at the front seat was made as narrow as could be without sacrificing leg room. The windows on each side of the pilot's station at the floor line afforded a view of the area ahead and below the aircraft. This was particularly useful during steep or vertical approaches possible with the autogiro. All windows, except those two at floor line were of laminated safety glass. The two higher windows at the pilot's right and left were raised and lowered by automobile-type window cranks. All other windows were fitted with rubber channels and sealed with non-hardening composition. The manufacturer boasted that the "upholstery was luxurious following the trends of the highest class automobiles." A careful study was made of springing and stuffing materials, seating angles and back shapes. The

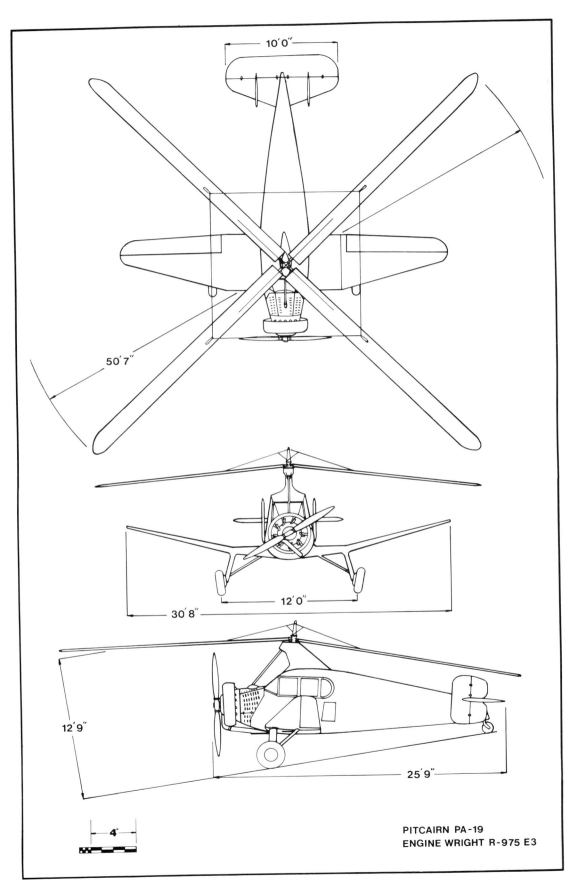

10′ 0″

50′ 7″

30′ 8″

12′ 0″

12′ 9″

25′ 9″

4′

PITCAIRN PA-19
ENGINE WRIGHT R-975 E3

52

pilot's seat was adjustable fore and aft. The co-pilot's seat was not adjustable, but had provision for bolting down to the structure at varying positions relative to the controls. The rear seat was forty-one and one-half inches wide. All the space in the fuselage wall, under the floor and on top of the cabin was packed with "Dry Zero" blanketing, the most efficient soundproofing and heat insulating material known in its day. Ventilators provided a continuous circulation of air, if desired, eliminating the need for opening the windows.

The instrument panel was finished to match the upholstery theme. The instrument complement included: altimeter, compass, air speed indicator, bank and turn, rate of climb, engine tachometer, electric rotor tachometer, electric fuel quantity gauge, oil pressure gauge, fuel pressure gauge, oil temperature and cylinder temperature, a clock and the company announced "an oil measuring rod accessible in flight." All the instruments could be serviced or replaced through a removable panel in the cowling ahead of the windshield and above the instruments. The control handles for the rotor clutch, rotor brake and parking brake, etc., were located in the instrument panel at its lower edge.

The control wheel and yoke were of the throw-over type so that the control could be passed to the copilot at will. The copilot's rudder pedals were folded back onto the floor and latched down with spring catches when they were not in use. All control cables were brought close together at the fuselage centerline and directed aft of the aircraft through a tunnel under the floor. Access was provided at most any point for servicing or replacement through screwed-down panels. The cables were not connected directly to the control surfaces which they control, rather they were connected to torque tubes within the fuselage which were in turn connected to the rudders or elevators.

The wing was of cantilever design and made in three basic panels. The centersection was approximately ten feet in span. Its wing chord was parallel, but the thickness tapered from the fuselage outward toward the outer panel attachment. The construction of the centersection was welded steel tubing. Two built-up welded steel tube trusses formed the front and rear spars. These were heat treated after welding. The drag braces were steel tubes which were welded into sockets made from larger size tubes which had been welded to the spar caps during the spar manufacture. The drag bracing was not heat treated.

The detachable outer panels were built up on a single wooden box spar carrying the aileron on its rear face. The inboard end was attached to the rear spar of the centersection with two bolts.

A system of ribs and drag braces formed the rest of the wing panel which was entirely covered with spruce veneer. Doped balloon fabric then covered the entire wing. A fine, smooth finish was made on the doped surface. A single bolt attached the forward part of the wing to the

PA-19 cabin head-on view.

(Pitcairn Photo)

centersection front spar. Large ailerons with what Pitcairn describes as a "specially shaped leading edge ahead of the hinge line" provided lateral control. This was, of course, similar to the Frieze-type surfaces now in general use but were new and novel at that time. These would provide, Pitcairn goes on, "powerful control at low speeds without being overly-sensitive at high speeds."

An independent tripod landing gear was attached to each side of the wing centersection providing a wheel tread of 12 feet. All attachments to the centersection were fixed. The wheel axles were attached to the oleo pistons which were cantilever and gave a nine-inch travel to absorb landing shocks. Tires were 9.5x12 "semi-balloon." A constant camber of the wheels was possible throughout the entire nine-inch travel. A smaller oleo strut with a full-swiveling wheel was attached to the rear of the fuselage.

The tail surface group was indeed unique and simple. The main member was a one-piece horizontal stabilizer assembly which was placed across the top of the upper longerons and bolted down. Construction was a wood frame with fabric covering. The elevator too was a single piece; this, however, of welded steel tubing with fabric cover. This was attached to the rear of the stabilizer through cast aluminum bearing blocks which were split to permit insertion of the elevator spar tube. Excess wear was taken out by filing or planing the mating faces of these blocks.

The vertical stabilizers were of welded steel tube construction, fabric covered. These were attached to the horizontal stabilizer at the leading edge and the front spar. The rudders, too, were of welded steel tubes attached to the rear of the vertical stabilizer both above and below the horizontal stabilizer. This particular tail configuration was chosen to offer the lowest profile, therefore offering good rotor clearance and to permit the vertical surfaces to operate in undisturbed air flow, clear of the fuselage.

The engine installed was a Wright R-975 E2 delivering 420 hp at 2150 rpm. Consideration was given to modifying the fuselage and/or the engine mount to accommodate the Pratt and Whitney Wasp "Junior," but no PA-19 was built with the P&W. An electric starter operated by a switch was similar to the automobiles of the day. The battery was installed in the fuselage aft of the cabin and was accessible through an outside door. Either hot or cold air could be diverted over the oil cooler as desired. Fuel was carried below the cabin floor in two tanks totaling 90 gallons. The front tank employed the familiar "stand pipe" arrangement, reserving a six-gallon emergency supply. The propeller installed was a ground-adjustable Hamilton Standard, although the literature promised that a controllable pitch propeller could be installed and the cruising speed would be improved by seven miles an hour.

The rotor blades were built in the same manner as the blades for the PCA-2 series; in fact, the blade attachments were interchangeable. The

3/4 front view of PA-19   *(Pitcairn Photo)*

54

Right side of Pitcairn PA-19 cabin autogiro. (Pitcairn Photo)

Left side view of Pitcairn PA-19 420 Hp, 5 place cabin autogiro. (Pitcairn Photo)

Although he reached the greatest altitude ever attained by man in his stratosphere, more than 10 miles above the earth. Prof. August Piccard today had his first airplane ride, in a cabin model autogiro, flown by James G. Ray, from the Washington Hoover Airport.

(Underwood Photo)

blade chord and the airfoil were also identical. The PA-19 blades were merely longer by approximately one and one half feet than the PCA-2. In the assembly of the rotor system the same familiar droop and interblade cables were evident.

The entire aircraft with the exception of the areas normally cowled with metal was fabric covered. The finish was hand rubbed to a mirror-like gloss, providing a smooth, easy-to-care-for surface. No standard paint scheme was offered.

For the first time in autogiros a complete electrical system was available as standard. It consisted of an engine-driven generator, electric starter, position lights and cabin lights, and landing lights. Bonding and shielding for radio were optional items.

Four were complete; two found their way to England. The PA-19 was indeed a beautiful aircraft.

In Volume 6 of "U.S. Civil Aircraft" the author, Joe Juptner offers a fine tribute to the Pitcairn PA-19 Autogiro: "With such credentials the Pitcairn PA -19 took its place on the market of 1933; based on its ability and its outstanding utility the PA-19 should have found instant favor, but being confronted with the depths of a national depression was more than a craft of this type could bargain for. There was a token in-

terest, of sorts, but financial difficulty at the Pitcairn plant finally halted its production and further development. Actually, the cabin-type PA-19 was an aircraft too far ahead of its time."

Specification and performance were reported as follows:

Gross weight	4035 lbs.
Empty weight	2675 lbs.
Useful load	1360 lbs

These figures are from a factory brochure and again do not agree with the CAA Approved Data.

Cruising speed	"over 100 mph"
add 7mph for controllable prop.	
High speed	125 mph
Landing speed	0 mph
Min descent speed at 27 mph	16 ft./sec.
Takeoff distance, no wind	270 ft.

"CAA AIRCRAFT LISTING"
PITCAIRN PA-19, 4 PCLAg,
ATC 509

Engine	Wright R-975E-2 420 hp
Fuel	90 gals.
Oil	8 gals.
No. pass.	3
Baggage	80 lbs.
Standard weight	4129 lbs.
	(See NOTE 1)

The front seats of the Pitcairn PA-19. The control column is a Waco cabin control unit. (Pitcairn Photo)

Interior of Pitcairn PA-19 cabin autogiro. (Pitcairn Photo)

Spec. basis   Approved Type Certificate No. 509

Serial Nos.   H-84 and up mfrd. prior to 9-30-39 eligible. Approval expired as of that date. (See NOTE 2)

Class I equipment: Battery 39 lbs.; Starter 30 lbs.; Generator 13 lbs.; Heater 5 lbs.; Propeller-adj. metal.

Class III equipment: Landing lights 15 lbs.; Flares (three 1 minute) 11 lbs.; Extra door 17 lbs.; Extra walk-way 15 lbs.; Elevator tab control 12 lbs.; Larger oil cooler 10 lbs.; Increase in weight of upholstery 8 lbs.; "Y" type control column, no change in weight; Propeller—controllable metal (Hm. Std. hub 2D30, blades 6101-6, low pitch setting 16°), net increase 60 lbs.

NOTE I. Serial No. H-84 is same as production model except shock absorbers, fixed wing, pylon structure, ailerons, and rear section of fuselage. Maximum standard weight 4097 lbs.

A PA-19 that found its way to England.   *("Flight" Magazine Photo)*

PA-19 making landing approach.   *(Flight Magazine Photo)*

Pitcairn PA-22

Pitcairn PA-22 in, perhaps, its original configuration.

(Pitcairn Photo)

In April of 1933 the Pitcairn organization began working on a new type of autogiro. This type promised to erase all the shortcomings of previous autogiros.

This autogiro incorporated "direct control"; a term which meant that the machine was controlled directly by the rotor, not depending on air speed for control sensitivity. As long as the rotor turned, the control was positive. Control was affected by tilting the rotor axis in the direction that control was wanted. Control response was equally good from the PA-22's high speed of 105 mph down to zero air speed. It was necessary to maintain only 12 mph in order to maintain altitude.

The PA-22 was a departure from normal four-bladed rotor to a three-bladed system in which the blades could be folded back over the fuselage for more convenient storage.

The real success of the machine must be credited to a British seven-cylinder radial 90 hp Pobjoy "Niagra" engine. This engine was geared .47 to 1 and delivered its power at 3500 rpm guaranteeing 84 hp at 3200 rpm. This permitted use of a large-diameter propeller for quick acceleration. Although designed as a two-placed side-by-side machine, Big Jim Ray, Pitcairn's chief test pilot, took more than half its cabin space.

The control stick hung from the center of the roof and had to be pushed forward on the ground into a stick lock when the rotor rpm slowed below a speed that kept it gyroscopically stable. On run up for takeoff it was kept locked until enough rpm was attained to keep it from tumbling like a run down top, chopping at the fuselage. Another new feature was introduced with the PA-22 was "jump takeoff."

Prior to takeoff the rotor could be run up to about 150% of normal RPM with the blades held in a no-lift position. By releasing a clutch mechanism the pilot could simultaneously transfer full power from the rotor to the tractor propeller with the blades assuming flight pitch of about three degrees. The energy stored in the over-reved rotor was translated into lift and the Autogiro took off vertically. As the rotor RPM died off to normal the propeller pulled the craft into a normal climbing attitude. When the meteorological conditions were right a vertical jump to eight to ten feet was not unusual.

A normal takeoff could be made by running the rotor up to nearly cruising speed than disengaging the engine from the rotor, opening the

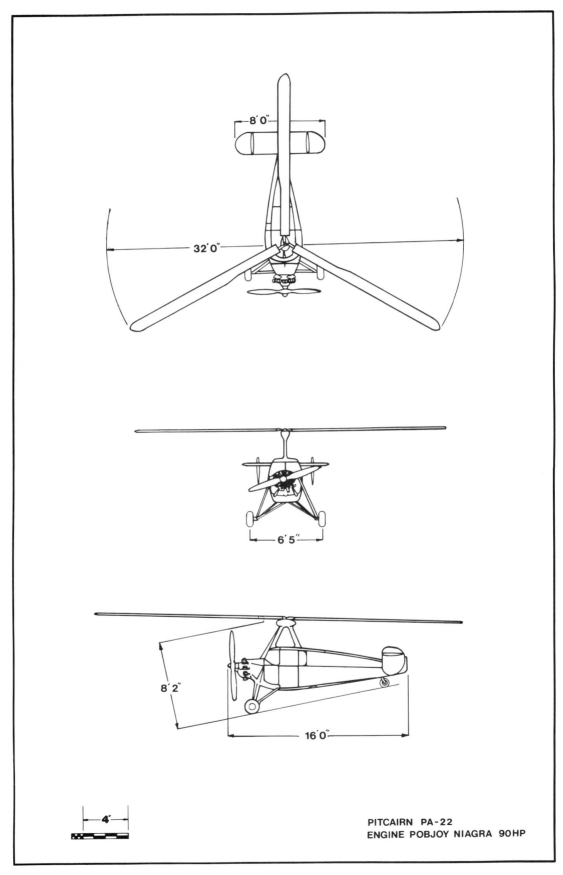

8' 0"

32' 0"

6' 5"

8' 2"

16' 0"

4"

PITCAIRN PA-22
ENGINE POBJOY NIAGRA 90HP

60

Rotor head for Pitcairn PA-22. The hose going from the center of the hub allows hydraulic fluid to operate a cylinder which decreases the rotor pitch for run-up and suddenly increases it for "jump take-off." Each blade will have a cylinder and a hose from the hub when complete. *(Pitcairn Photo)*

throttle all the way and lifting off after a very short ground run. The engine could not be used to power the rotor during takeoff because an anti-torque device would be needed to prevent the fuselage from turning in the opposite direction as the rotor due to engine torque.

The fuselage was made from gas welded steel tubes of varying diameters and wall thicknesses. It was fabric covered with the exception of the generous allocation of transparent material around the cockpit.

Because the rotor provided all the lift and all the longitudinal and lateral control, wings were not necessary. A small rudder on the rear of the fuselage would tighten the turning radius, however, turns would be made in either direction by merely rolling into a left or right bank.

Blades were similar to earlier models but the droop and interblade cables were no longer necessary due to improvements in blade design and construction.

The smaller autogiro was a test bed for many ideas—the landing gear, tail and rotor system took on many shapes. At one time, a single large wheel was used under the center of the fuselage with small castering wheels forward. The rotor, at one time had hinges near the center of rotation as well as about half way between the blade root and the tip. Apparently this idea did not offer enough improvement in performance or rotor smoothness to justify the expense of manufacturing the double hinged blades. Specifications were as follows:

Specifications

Gross weight	1140 lbs.
Empty weight	600 lbs.
Top speed	107 mph
Cruise speed	90 mph
Landing speed	0 mph

Pitcairn PA-22 with blades folded for storage. *(Pitcairn Photo)*

Pitcairn PA-33 and PA-34

1935 Pitcairn Observation Autogiro PA-33 Army YG-2.   *(Pitcairn Photo)*

These autogiros were similar to each other in nearly all appearances except the landing gear.

There had been a persistent rumor that the PA-33 and PA-34 were greatly modified XO-P-1 and YG-1 autogiros which were returned to Pitcairn for this rework.

During a search of the archives for more pictures of the YG-2 and XOP-2 autogiros a picture of the fuselage skeleton for the XOP-2 was uncovered. It could easily be seen that there was no resemblance of the XOP-1 (PCA-2) to the XOP-1 skeleton.

The design differences between the earlier Pitcairn-built Army and Navy autogiros were: A direct control rotor system using only three blades with fifty-foot diameter and absence of all the supporting and interblade wires. The engine was a Wright R-975 producing 450 hp turning a Hamilton Standard two-position propeller. A full N.A.C.A. cowl was used over the engine for cooling. A rotor pylon similar to the one used on the PA-18 was installed, having two large-diameter tubes on the fuselage centerline, braced to the upper longerons with streamlined tie rods. Gross weight was increased to 3300 lbs.

Two XOP-2s were delivered to the US Navy and the Army Air Corps purchased one YG-2. The only difference in the two models seems to be the landing gear.

The rumor may have belonged to the PA-39s which were made from PA-18s.

Pitcairn PA-34 (XOP-2) Navy autogiro. The same as PA-34 (YG-2) except landing gear. (National Archives Photo)

Pitcairn PA-34 Navy XOP-2 Autogiro. (Pitcairn Photo)

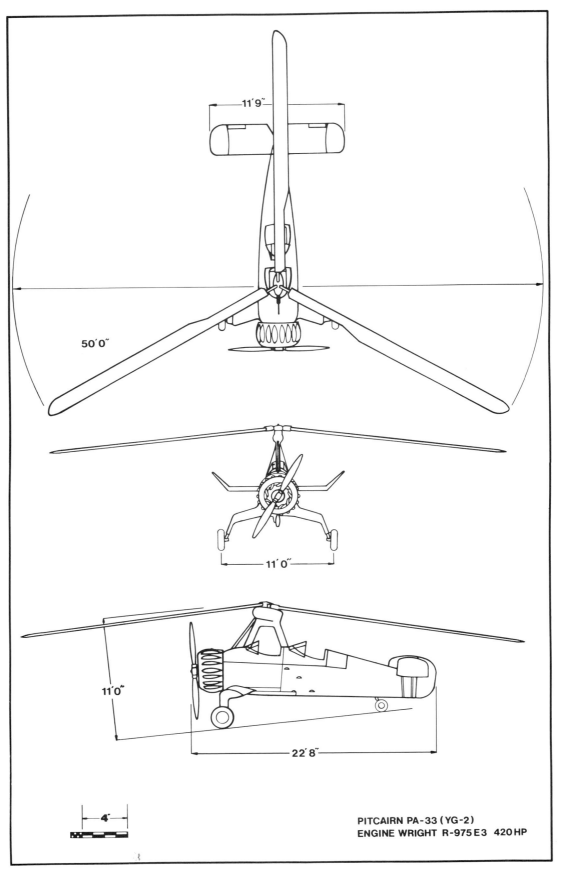

11′9″

50′0″

11′0″

11′0″

22′8″

4″

PITCAIRN PA-33 (YG-2)
ENGINE WRIGHT R-975 E3 420 HP

Pitcairn PA-33 (YG-2) Autogiro. (Pitcairn Photo)

Pitcairn PA-33 Navy XOP-2. (Pitcairn Photo)

Pitcairn PA-33 (YG-2). Note pitot-static tube at rotor head, different landing gear. (Pitcairn Photo)

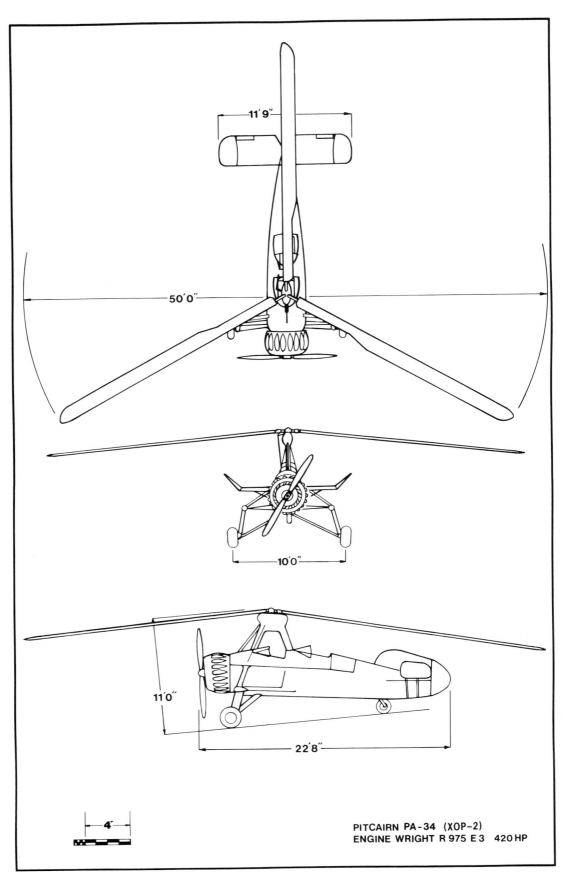

11'9"

50'0"

10'0"

11'0"

22'8"

4'

PITCAIRN PA-34 (XOP-2)
ENGINE WRIGHT R 975 E 3   420 HP

Pitcairn PA-33 (YG-2) flying over the Delaware River at Philadelphia.

(Aero Service Photo)

Pitcairn PA-35 (or AC-35)

Pitcairn's AC-35 with Jim Ray in cockpit running tests on front wheel steering. Pobjoy "Niagra" engine can be seen behind cockpit.
(Pitcairn Photo)

In 1936 the U.S. Bureau of Air Commerce bought a two-placed autogiro; this too used a Pobjoy "Niagra" 90 hp engine.

In order to give the occupants more forward visibility, the engine was mounted just behind the seats with a shaft running through the cabin to the propeller on the nose. With this unorthodox engine installation, it was necessary to fancool the engine as all piston engines in helicopters are now cooled. The engine could also be connected to the rear wheel to drive the autogiro along the road with the rotor blades folded back over the tail and the propeller disconnected from the engine. This craft can now be seen in the National Air Museum's Silver Hill Facility or as it is properly know, "The Paul E. Garber Facility." There was some confusion as to the proper model number being called the PA-35 or the AC-35.

Pitcairn AC-35 contrarotating propellers can be seen clearly. Pobjoy "Niagra" 90 hp was the engine mounted aft and was fan cooled.   *(Pitcairn Photo)*

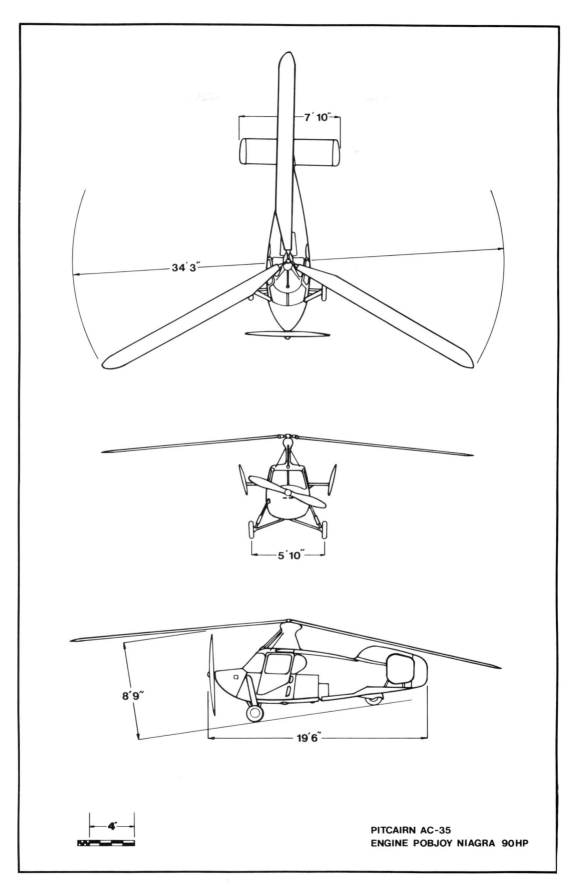

7′10″

34′3″

5′10″

8′9″

19′6″

4″

PITCAIRN AC-35
ENGINE POBJOY NIAGRA 90HP

Pitcairn AC-35 with one large propeller replacing two smaller contrarotating ones and stationary vanes behind the propellers.
(Pitcairn Photo)

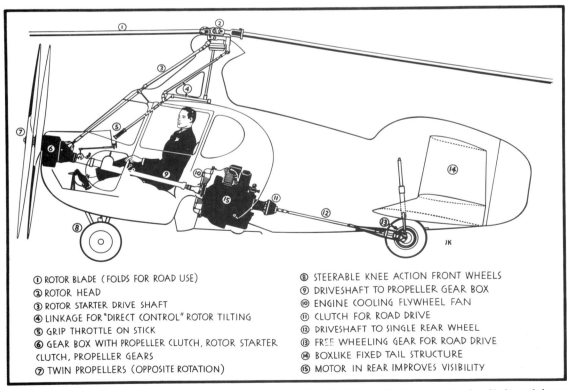

① ROTOR BLADE (FOLDS FOR ROAD USE)
② ROTOR HEAD
③ ROTOR STARTER DRIVE SHAFT
④ LINKAGE FOR "DIRECT CONTROL" ROTOR TILTING
⑤ GRIP THROTTLE ON STICK
⑥ GEAR BOX WITH PROPELLER CLUTCH, ROTOR STARTER CLUTCH, PROPELLER GEARS
⑦ TWIN PROPELLERS (OPPOSITE ROTATION)

⑧ STEERABLE KNEE ACTION FRONT WHEELS
⑨ DRIVESHAFT TO PROPELLER GEAR BOX
⑩ ENGINE COOLING FLYWHEEL FAN
⑪ CLUTCH FOR ROAD DRIVE
⑫ DRIVESHAFT TO SINGLE REAR WHEEL
⑬ FREE WHEELING GEAR FOR ROAD DRIVE
⑭ BOXLIKE FIXED TAIL STRUCTURE
⑮ MOTOR IN REAR IMPROVES VISIBILITY

Pitcairn AC-35 drive and control diagram. Note two contrarotating propellers. The dual propeller feature was abandoned in favor of a larger single propeller because a report says, "Propellers set up a howl that would shatter glass."
(Pitcairn Photo)

Skyway Engineering version (in the late '50s) of Pitcairn's AC-35. Probably only the rotor system of the original AC-35 was retained.

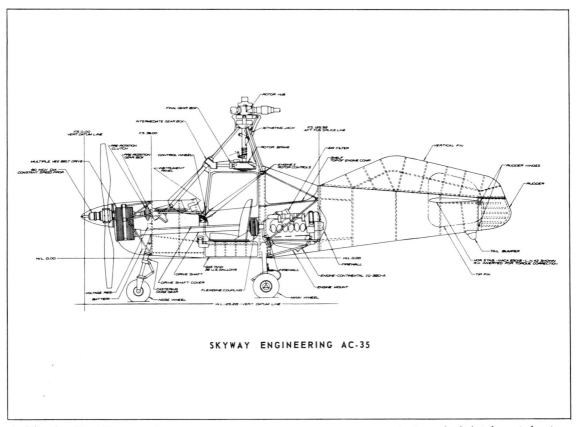

SKYWAY ENGINEERING AC-35

An inboard profile of Skyway Engineering's version of Pitcairn's AC-35. The drive system is shown clearly but the control system does not show.

Skyway engineering AC-35's.

(Pitcairn Photo)

Pitcairn PA-36

Pitcairn PA-36 showing "buried" engine installation, Harold F. Pitcairn stepping out. Note four-bladed propeller turning in the opposite direction to the U.S. norm.
(Philadelphia Ledger Photo)

The PA-36 was possibly the most beautiful autogiro ever built. It was the last autogiro built and designed by the original Pitcairn group.

The fuselage was crafted from gleaming sheet aluminum. Pitcairn had no experience with this type of construction, so fuselages for two PA-36s were built by Luscombe Airplane Company who at that time was located in nearby Trenton, New Jersey.

The PA-36 began flying in 1939, most of the early flying was done by Lew Leavitt who had been chief test pilot for Kellett Autogiro Company. Later Fred "Slim" Soule took over when Lew went to Platt LePage Helicopter Company to fly the XR-1. The forward landing gear on the PA-36 was steerable for use when the autogiro was driven over the road.

The powerplant in this craft was a 165 hp Warner Super Scarab. This engine was mount-

ed in the fuselage, aft of the cabin as in the PA-35. It was necessary to cool it with a fan. It might be suspected that the work done on cooling this engine with a fan can be credited with some of the success of the Sikorsky R-4 helicopter, which later used the same engine. Sikorsky had signed up about that time as a licensee of Autogiro Company of America to take advantage of some of the Pitcairn rotor systems and rotor control patents.

The blades were similar to the earlier autogiros with some exceptions. The blades were tapered in thickness and plan shape. The main members were the usual heat treated steel tube. These were different in that they were not round but elliptical in shape and were tapered from the inboard end to the tip. They also changed in wall thickness from heavy at the inboard to light at the tip. If the spar had a constant taper from root

73

Pitcairn PA-36 at Pitcairn Factory. The beautiful fuselage was built for Pitcairn by Luscombe Airplane Co., Trenton, New Jersey.
(Pitcairn Photo)

Pitcairn's PA-36 landing at Pitcairn Field. The water tower and hangar are still on the field, which is now Willow Grove Naval Air Station.
(Pitcairn Photo)

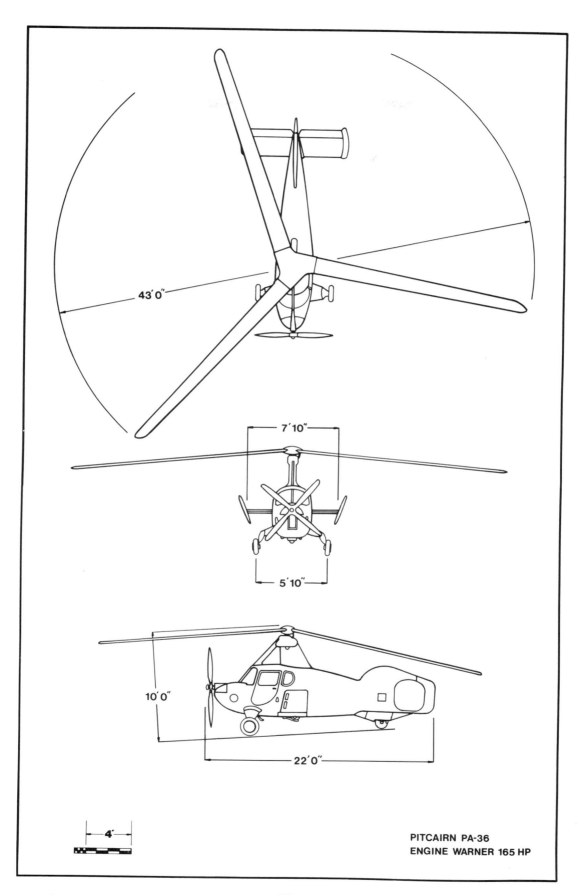

43´ 0˝

7´ 10˝

5´ 10˝

10´ 0˝

22´ 0˝

4´

PITCAIRN PA-36
ENGINE WARNER 165 HP

Pitcairn PA-36 at the top of a "jump takeoff." The jump is made with no power going to the rotor. (Pitcairn Photo)

to tip, each of the collars that attached the ribs to the spar would have to be different. Instead of this, the spars were tapered in steps, so that 15 or 20 ribs could be the same in each blade before another size collar was needed. The blades were fabric covered. There was no CAA Type Certificate obtained for this model. No production was undertaken. Only one of the PA-36s flew. The

effort was suspended when the company became Pitcairn-Larsen Autogiro Company. It stayed in business long enough to build the PA-39s and help G&A Aircraft Co. to get the PA-39s started (G&A was AGA for a short time during this time they built Waco troop gliders in production for the Air Corps.)

Agnew Larson, left and Harold Pitcairn, right, examining the rotor head of the PA-36. (Pitcairn Photo)

Pitcairn PA 36 with Fred "Slim" Soule at the controls. Slim was Pitcairn's test pilot through most of the PA-22, All the AC-35, PA 33, PA 34, PA 39 and XO 61 in addition to the PA 36 work. (Pitcairn Photo)

Pitcairn PA-39

Pitcairn PA-39—six were "built" for the British Military from Pitcairn PA-18 autogiros bought back from customers. Wings were removed, horizontal tail replaced and a "direct control" rotor system installed. The Kinner engine and fixed pitch propeller were replaced with Warner "Super Scarab" and constant-speed propeller. (Pitcairn Photo)

About 1941, Harold Pitcairn ceased manufacturing Autogiros. Pitcairn's airfield was acquired by the Navy after an appraisal by real estate experts on the basis of the value of open land. Pitcairn maintained the licensing organization, Autogiro Company of America, and continued as a small group having an office in Jenkintown, Pennsylvania, near Willow Grove.

Paul Stanley, who had joined the Pitcairn organization when the Cierva C-8 came to Willow Grove, was retained as chief engineer. He was assisted by Gage Tidd and Harris "Pat" Campbell, both were excellent mechanical engineers.

The autogiro manufacturing firm became A.G.A. for "Autogiros, Gliders and Airplanes." The name changed to G&A, then Firestone Tire and Rubber Company took over and continued to operate at G&A, a division of Firestone Tire and Rubber Company.

Some of the Pitcairn personnel joined AGA and continued on to Firestone. Agnew Larsen was one of those. At the beginning of World War II, the British government was looking for an aircraft that could be carried aboard ship in a convoy and could be launched and recovered while the convoy was under way. The purpose was to scout for submarines which were taking their

toll of English vessels en route with war supplies.

Helicopters were not yet available, so an autogiro was considered. G&A was approached and they proposed a two-place, open cockpit autogiro, using a 165 Warner Super Scarab turning a two-bladed, constant-speed propeller. The model was a PA-39.

The PA-39s were ordered from the Pitcairn organization because of the British-owned Cierva Autogiro Company. The British were using all their aircraft building capacity to produce fighter planes to defend England that is why they turned to Pitcairn for the autogiros. Wing Commander Reggie Brie, a former Cierva Test pilot was the British supervisor for the project.

Because construction materials were critical it was decided to use the PA-18 airframe as a basis for the PA-39.

Seven PA-18s were bought back from their owners, who could, in most cases not use them because of severe restrictions put on private flying during the war.

The only parts actually retained were the fuselage, rotor, pylon, vertical tail, tail wheel, main wheels and brakes. First consideration was to use the Kinner R-5, 165hp original equipment

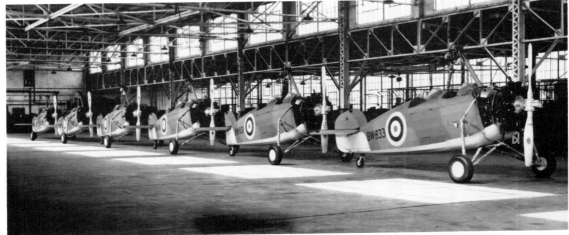

The production line of PA-39 autogiros inside Pitcairn's factory.

(Pitcairn Photo)

Pitcairn PA-39 rear cockpit.

(Pitcairn Photo)

Pitcairn PA-39 pylon, controls and rotor blades. Notice pylon is the same as wire-braced two-strut PA-18 pylon.

(Warren Ship Photo)

engine, but this engine had a tapered crankshaft at the propeller hub and would not accept a constant speed propeller.

Because the rotor was to provide the control of the PA-39 as in the PA-22, 35 and 36, the wings were removed. A new type horizontal tail was designed with slanted vertical pieces referred to as "tip shields."

The rotor head was the same as the PA-36 and was equipped for vertical "jump" takeoff, so the PA-39 could be taken off with no horizontal roll. This feature backed up with a landing speed of zero mph made it a natural for operation from a makeshift flight deck aboard an ocean freighter, to look for Nazi submarines.

Seven were completed. One was retained by Pitcairn for installation of rockets in the tips of the rotor blades. The purpose was to take off with a powered rotor. Using rockets at the blade

Front view Pitcairn PA-39.

(Warren Ship Photo)

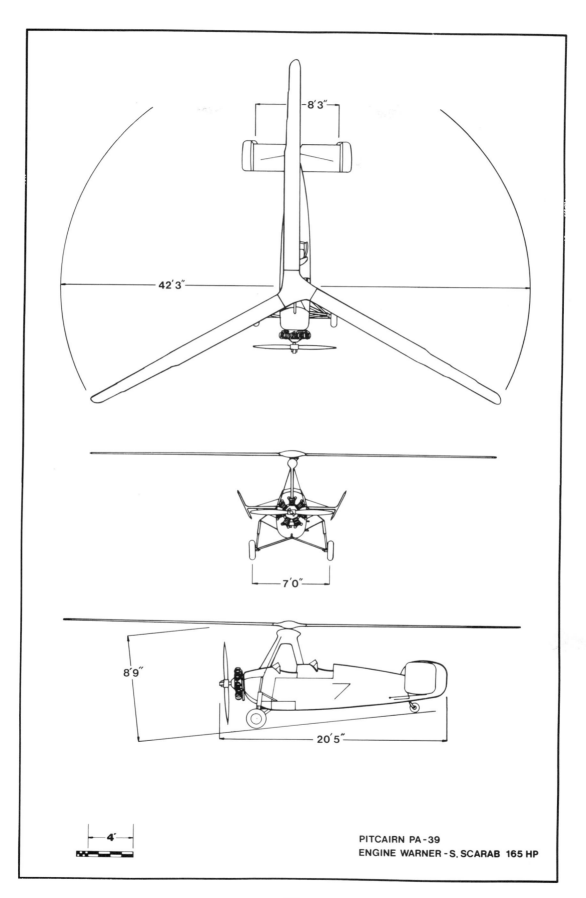

8'3"

42'3"

7'0"

8'9"

20'5"

4'

PITCAIRN PA-39
ENGINE WARNER - S. SCARAB 165 HP

tips causes no torque, eliminating the need for an anti-torque rotor. Rocket drive is expensive to operate but no transmission is needed, so the system possibly could be built quite a bit cheaper. Planned flight experiments never came off. The autogiro was donated to Princeton University's Forrestall Research Center. Princeton University never flew it. About 1959, it was sold to one of their mechanics who assembled it and John Miller, one of Kellett's former test pilots, flew it. Later it was used by Umbaugh Aircraft when they were first promoting their gyroplane. Their test pilot was Fred "Slim" Soule who had flown all the PA-39s originally. Then it was bought by Ryan Aeronautical of San Diego. It was badly damaged in a landing accident there. It has since moved through several owners and the son of Harold Pitcairn, Stephen Pitcairn, owns it and is repairing it.

The remaining PA-39s were shipped to England, luckily on two separate vessels. One ship was sunk en route by the very submarines that the PA-39s were later to seek out.

The jump takeoff or self-catapulting feature was the same as the PA-36. The blades were set at zero lift angle and the rotor was run up to 285 rpm when the pitch angle was hydraulically changed to 3½ degrees. The rpm then bled off to about 170 rpm as the autogiro climbed. A jump to about 15 feet could be made on the right day.

Lateral and longitudinal control was effected by tilting the rotor axis in the direction that control was desired. A control column with a steering wheel at its top was moved forward and backward for longitudinal control and was rolled left or right for lateral control. A small rudder at the rear of the fuselage would shorten the turning radius. A turn could be made by banking the autogiro right or left with the control wheel.

The original design, which was not built, with a Kinner R-5 engine was shown with a 40-foot diameter constant tapered blade, while the Warner Super Scarab version that was built had a 42-foot diameter step-tapered rotor.

Specifications

Gross weight	1996.5
Empty weight	1482.5
Top speed	110 mph
Minimum speed	15 mph
Landing speed	0 mph

Pitcairn PA-39 tail.   *(Warren Ship Photo)*

PA-39 Front Section.   *(Warren Ship Photo)*

Alfaro

The Alfaro Autogiro built under contract between Pitcairn and Heraclio Alfaro who had designed it. Alfaro had an impressive record as an engineer and designed a radial engine with opposed cylinders turning a "wobble" plate which turned the propeller shaft. It can be seen in the Franklin Institute, Philadelphia, Pennsylvania. Heraclio had given Harold Pitcairn a letter of introduction to Cierva. (Pitcairn Photo)

On January 12, 1929, Harold Pitcairn entered into a contract with Heraclio Alfaro, the man who had given him a letter of introduction to Cierva. Alfaro had proposed a light, three-place open cockpit autogiro. He had previously done some notable work with fixed-wing aircraft and had assisted in the design of the Pescara Helicopter.

Pitcairn originally designated the Alfaro machine PCA-2-30. Later it was designated the PA-11.

One novel feature was a Formica covered rotor blade. Formica was the '30s version of plastic. The blades were designed and built by the Formica Company.

The fuselage was a conventional welded steel tube structure with fabric covering.

The landing gear had a wide tread but was simpler than Pitcairn's designs. A vertical cabane structure was wire-braced to the lower longerons. A welded "vee" assembly went from this cabane to the lower end of the shock struts.

The wings and ailerons were Formica covered and were wire-braced to the fuselage. The wire bracing actually completed the landing gear structure. The wing tips were turned up as in Pitcairn's early models. The horizontal stabil-izer was wood with Micarta cover as was the rudder. The vertical fin was steel welded tubing covered with fabric.

Design was begun July 17, 1929, construction work began in November 1929 and was completed July 18, 1930. Just a year from the signing of the contract the first flight was August 18, 1930.

The autogiro was on its way from Willow Grove to the National Air Races in Cleveland, Ohio in August of 1930. For some unknown reason its pilot, J. Paul (Skip) Lukens landed in a farmer's field in Butler, Pennsylvania to stay over night. On takeoff on August 21, 1930 it struck a stone wall and was destroyed. Lukens was not injured.

The reported cause of the accident was the weight of condensed moisture inside the Micarta covered rotor blades causing them not to attain the proper rpm for takeoff.

Although Alfaro proposed rebuilding the craft, Pitcairn declined.

Specifications

Gross weight	1813 lbs.
Empty weight	1283 lbs.

The powerplant was a Warner Scarab, seven cylinder radial engine giving 110 hp.

Performance data is not available.

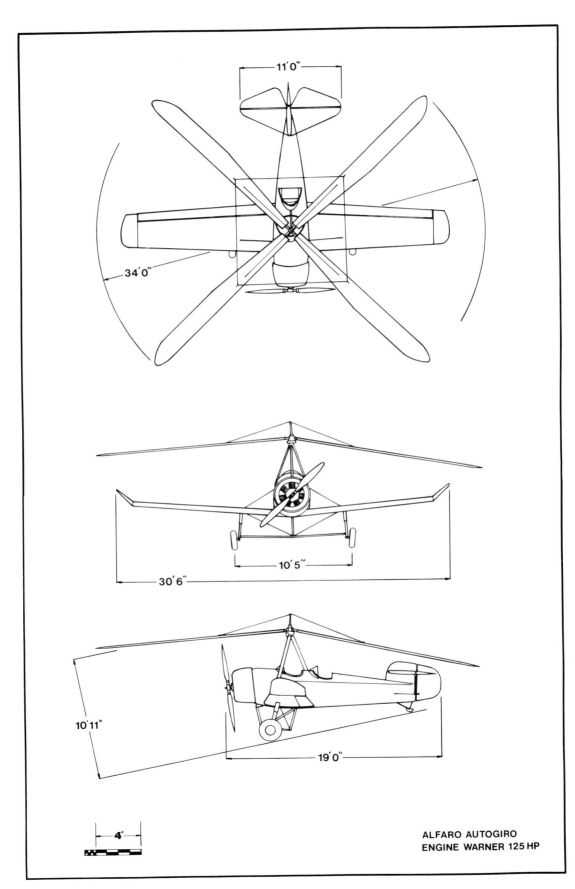

11′0″

34′0″

10′5″

30′6″

10′11″

19′0″

4′

ALFARO AUTOGIRO
ENGINE WARNER 125 HP

Alfaro Autogiro built by Heraclio Alfaro under contract to Pitcairn. (Pitcairn Photo)

Alfaro autogiro built under contract to Pitcairn. Destroyed on the way to Cleveland Air Races on August 21, 1930 when it hit a stone wall on takeoff from a farm field where the pilot left the craft all night.
(Pitcairn Photo)

Pitcairn YO-61

Pitcairn G&A YO-61 with Jacobs 300 hp engine. *(Pitcairn Photo)*

By 1942, the helicopter was a reality. Several were flying successfully. There was talk of production. There was still some interest in autogiros. Pitcairn proposed an autogiro which looked like a helicopter. The nose of the fuselage was transparent plastic. Generous sections of clear plastic were used in the doors and the roof. Space was provided for a pilot in the nose with an observer sitting directly behind him.

Power was from Jacobs 300 hp mounted in the pusher position. This plant turned a Hamilton Standard constant-speed propeller 102-inches in diameter.

The tail assembly was mounted on outriggers. The horizontal assembly was non-controllable with turned-up tips. There was a rudder and a vertical fin on the centerline of the aircraft. They seemed to be cambered deeply on one side to counteract the engine torque like the vertical fin on the Mailwing.

One was completed and flown extensively. The rotor hub was similar to the PA-36 and incorporated jump takeoff.

Specifications

Top speed	103 mph
Landing speed	0 mph
Gross weight	3038 lbs.

Buhl Aircraft of Marysville, Michigan became an autogiro licensee. Buhl had been a metal stamping company who went into aircraft manufacturing. They produced several airplanes from a light one-place mid-wing wire braced monoplane with a sheet metal fuselage to a 4 to 5-place sesqi-wing biplane.

Their autogiro design was a two-place, tandem seat open cockpit pusher. The engine was a 165 hp Continental 7-cylinder radial mounted in the pusher position.

The rotor hub was the hub used on the Pitcairn PAA-1, PA-18 series and the Kellett K2, K3, K4. Blades were PAA-1, PA-18 type, turning in the opposite direction. There has been some controversy concerning the diameter of the rotor, often reported as 48 feet. A letter dated July 14, 1931 from Roger Ward, production manager for Autogiro Specialties, acknowledges an order for a set of 40-foot diameter blades which would be the same as Pitcairn's PA-18.

This was the first pusher autogiro and quite far down the manufacturing path it was suddenly noticed that the rotor must rotate in opposite direction to tractor configuration or the natural rolling moment (due to advancing and retreating blades) would add to the engine torque. The wings and landing gear were similar to the PA-18.

It was reported to fly well, but no certification was undertaken.

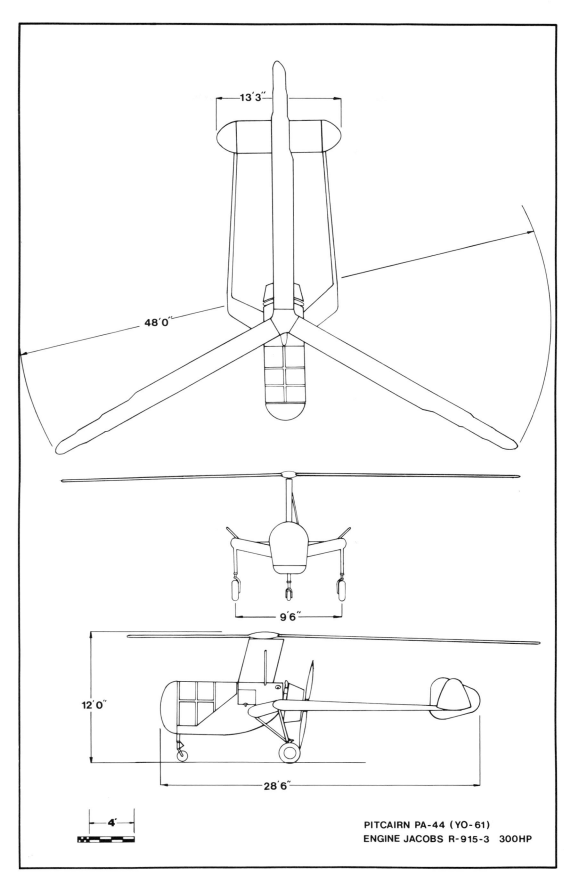

13'3"

48'0"

9'6"

12'0"

28'6"

4'

PITCAIRN PA-44 (YO-61)
ENGINE JACOBS R-915-3   300HP

Aerial shot of Buhl autogiro. (Smithsonian Photo)

Buhl autogiro in early 1932 with PCA-2 in background. This picture proves that Buhl rotor turned opposite.

(Smithsonian Photo)

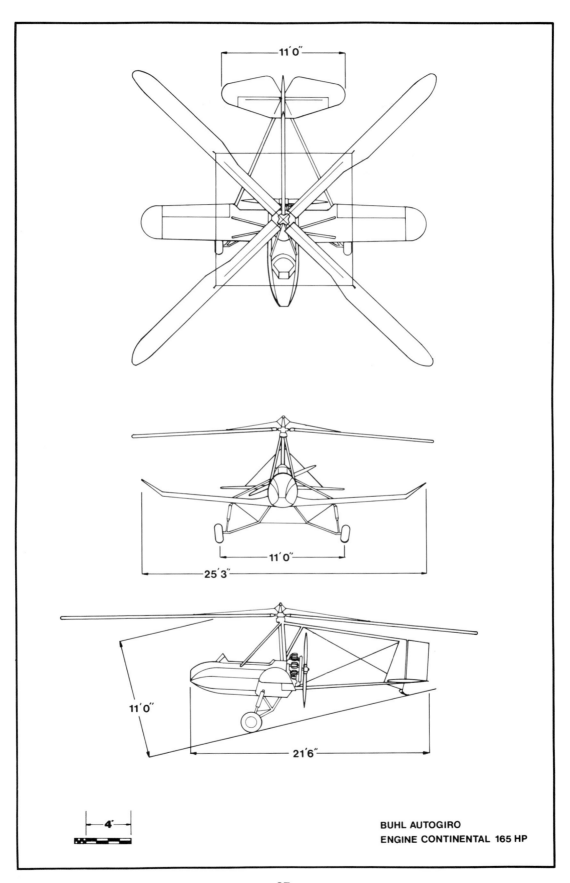

11'0"

11'0"

25'3"

11'0"

21'6"

4'

BUHL AUTOGIRO
ENGINE CONTINENTAL 165 HP

Kellett Autogiro Company

Autogiro inventor, pilots, engineers and manufacturers of the early autogiro. Left to right: Nick Luddington, officer of Kellett; Rod Kellett and Wallace Kellett of Kellett Aircraft; Harold Pitcairn, Pitcairn Autogiro; W. L. LePage, Chief Engineer, Kellett; Jim Ray, Test Pilot at Pitcairn; and Guy Miller, Test Pilot of Kellett in 1931 at Philadelphia. Shown standing on the Kellett autogiro is the autogiro inventor. Iuan De la Cierva. *(Kellett Photo)*

Kellett K1-X

The Kellett Brothers, Wallace and Rod, became interested in autogiros and obtained a license under the Autogiro Company of America.

Wallace had been a World War I aviator and after the war had sold French-built Farman airplanes in the United States.

Rather than use the proven Cierva or Pitcairn designs, they went their own way. Their entry was described by Kellett's Engineering Report No. 8 as an "extremely light, single-place experimental autogiro." It was designated the K1-X. The airframe was designed to receive any one of three rotor systems: a two-bladed rigid type, a three-bladed hinged type, or a four-bladed hinged type. The two-bladed type was the only one built. The original design was to use a 27-foot 6-inch diameter rotor, but the di-

ameter was increased to 32-feet 6-inches. This required lengthening the fuselage to permit the rotor to clear the vertical tail surfaces when it rotated.

The rotor was of wooden monocoque construction using a Göttingen 449 airfoil faired into a 40x12 inch center section. The rotor hub and bearings to permit the rotor to teeter like a seesaw were housed inside the center section.

The fuselage construction was spot welded stainless steel angles. The Budd Company, auto body builders in Philadelphia, who were pioneers in spot welding stainless steel aircraft structures built the fuselage.

The landing gear was made from welded steel tubing. The hydraulic shock struts had an 8-inch travel, using stacked rubber discs for taxiing. The wheels were equipped with 18x3 high pressure tires.

The wings were actually tail surfaces. All were of wood construction.

The entire autogiro except the rotor was covered with airplane fabric and doped.

The original powerplant was a Szekley (pronounced Zay-Kay) three cylinder, air cooled, radial engine giving 40 horsepower at 1800 rpm. This was changed during testing to a five cylin-

Kellett's first autogiro, the KI-X. This one never left the ground. Kellett turned to the Autogiro Company of America rotor systems when they became a licensee. This craft began with a 45 hp Szekley radial, then changed to 65 hp Lambert.   (Kellett Photo)

Another view of the K-1X with the Szekley engine.   (Kellett Photo)

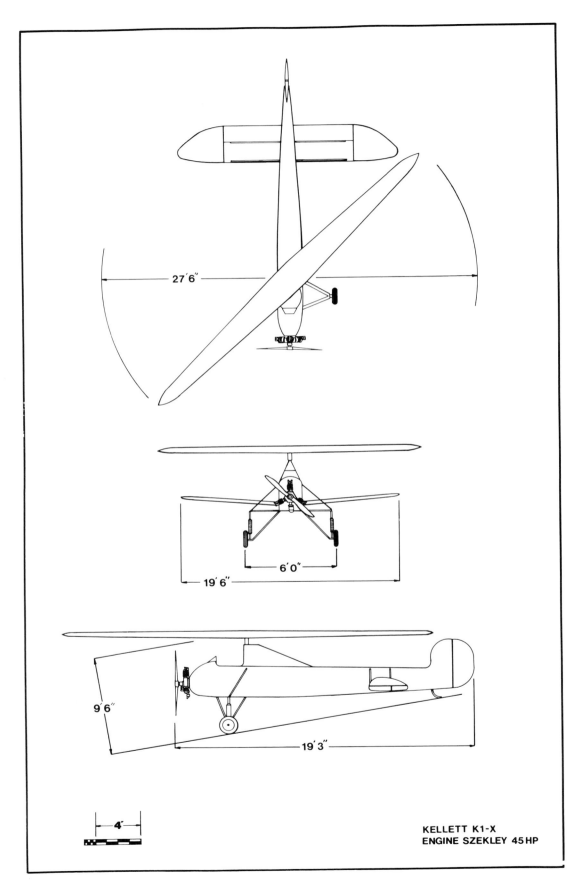

27′6″

19′6″

6′0″

9′6″

19′3″

4′

KELLETT K1-X
ENGINE SZEKLEY 45 HP

The Kellett KI-X rotor in front of a Krieder-Reisner Aircraft, (now Fairchild) where it was built.   *(Kellett Photo)*

Rear view of Kellett's first autogiro, model KI-X. It never flew.   *(Pitcairn Photo)*

der, air-cooled Velie M-5 radial engine giving 65 HP at 1900 rpm. The propeller for the Szekley was 6 feet in diameter. There is no record of the diameter propeller used on the Velie, but it is assumed to be the same diameter.

Tests began October 14, 1930, apparently at Philadelphia Municipal Airport, on October 15. The K1-X was moved to Pitcairn Field. Larger wheels from Pitcairn's Cierva C-19 were installed and the tail skid shortened 1-½ inches to increase the ground angle. The RH landing gear failed on the first run with these wheels. Reports show tests were discontinued on December 3, 1930. In spite of the fact that the 65 hp Velie was installed early in November 1930, the K1-X never left the ground.

Specifications

Gross weight	775 lbs.
Empty weight	545 lbs.*

*E. weight increased 87 lbs. with Velie engine.

Estimated performance with Szekley:

Maximum speed	65 mph
Minimum speed	N.A.
Absolete ceiling	6000 ft.
Taxi run for takeoff	200 ft.
Landing run	25 ft.
Vertical descent	14.5 feet per second
Rate of climb at 32 mph	250 ft. per minute

There was no means provided to spin the rotor up mechanically so all attempts to take off had to be made by taxiing faster and faster to build up rotor RPM. One straight run could not be made. Rpm was lost each time on turns and down wind runs. The final test report says, "Air speed 58 mph rotor 150 rpm—no tendency to take off. Broke tailskid Tests discontinued".

Kellett K1-X fuselage and landing gear.

(Kellett Photo)

Kellett K-2

K-2 autogiro used by steel pier in Atlantic City, an amusement pier.   (Kellett Photo)

Undaunted, Kellett went on to design a machine similar to the Pitcairn and Cierva style, which had been successful. The differences were that Kellet's was a side-by-side seater, had larger blade area and a much simpler landing gear.

The first flight was on April 24, 1931 by Jim Ray, Pitcairn's chief test pilot. Approval by the Department of Commerce (1931's FAA) was obtained under a "group 2" type certificate # 2-431 on May 27, 1931, just about a month after the first flight. Joe Juptner's Volume 5, shows K-2 having ATC 437. The Chief of the Department of Commerce, Gilbert Budwig, flew the K-2 and complained of lack of aileron control at low speeds and slow rate of climb. Flight test notes fail to show any corrective work done between flights. Approval was granted on the promise that the aileron control would be improved.

The Autogiro was flown to Washington for the evaluation by the Department of Commerce. A note on the test report says it took 3½ hours to fly from Philadelphia to Washington against a 20 mile per hour wind. The return trip required about two hours. The distance is about 130 miles.

The fuselage was gas welded of steel tubing using square tubes for longerons. It was lightly faired on the sides with deep fairing on the top with no fairing on the bottom.

A much simpler landing gear than the Pitcairn models was designed. A long-travel oleo shock strut was attached to the bottom of the wing at the front spar. The lower end was attached to the axle. A drag brace took the taxiing and aft loads. These were attached to a cabin assembly under the fuselage. The axle and drag braces faired into a streamline shape with balsa wood on the aft side which was wrapped with airplane fabric and doped.

The entire tail assembly was made from wood resulting in a very light structure. Spars were solid spruce, the ribs were light plywood web members with spruce cap strips and a few vertical members. The trailing edged of the rudder and elevators were round aluminum tubes which were pressed into a streamlined shape.

Wing beams were box spars with spruce longitudinal and vertical members. The web members were three-ply mahogany with a 45 degree face grain. Ash blocks were built into the spars at points of heavy loads. Most ribs were made of square spruce cap strips and diagonals; some were made with spruce cap strips and mahogany plywood members. The airfoil, a RAF 30 was symmetrical in shape.

The wings were braced to the fuselage with

93

Kellett K-2, Serial No. 1. This craft has a different turtle-deck behind the cockpit than the follow-on K-2 and K-3 had. (Pitcairn Photo)

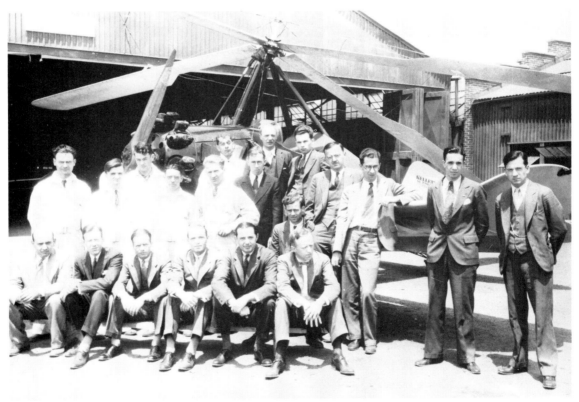

Kellett personnel in 1931 at factory in Philadelphia Municipal Airport. Top row: (in front of windshield) Elliot Daland, formerly of Huff-Daland; to the right of Daland is Chuck Miller. Middle row: Directly below Daland, Hugh Mulvey; seated directly below Miller, Ralph McClarren; Front row: third from left, Guy Miller, test pilot; Wallace Kellett; Rod Kellett; Unknown. Kellett K-2 autogiro in background. (Kellett Photo)

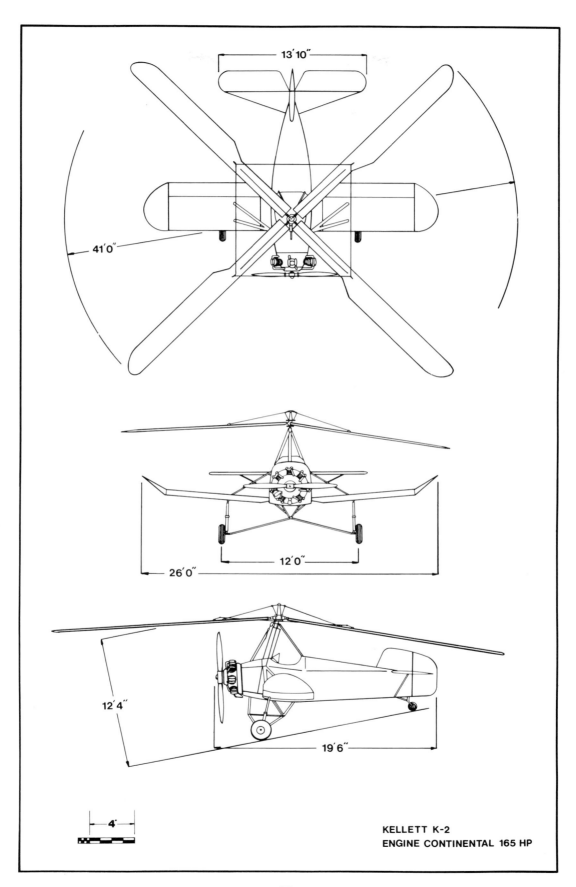

13' 10"

41' 0"

26' 0"

12' 0"

12' 4"

19' 6"

4'

KELLETT K-2
ENGINE CONTINENTAL 165 HP

95

Construction photos of the prototype Kellett K-2 autogiro.

(Kellett Photo)

Tail shock strut on Kellett K-2 and K-3 autogiros. (Kellett Photo)

Kellett K-2 engine and mount Continental R-670 160 hp. Note horseshoe shaped wood engine bearer. (Kellett Photo)

aluminum streamlined struts. The front spars carried the landing gear loads from the wing to the fuselage top longerons.

The entire autogiro including the rotor blades was fabric covered. The rotor system was similar to those used on the Pitcairn Autogiros with some exceptions. Most noticeable was the wider chord rotor blade; 23 inches instead of the 18 inches used on the Pitcairn blades of similar gross weight autogiros, keeping the same thickness ratio for the rotor airfoil. The steel tube spar was made from $2\frac{1}{8}$ inch diameter instead of the $1\frac{3}{4}$ on the Pitcairn light autogiros. This had a secondary importance in the method of assembly of the rib to the spar. Instead of employing the delicate process of spot welding the rib collars to the spar, Kellett pinned the collars using a 1/8" clevis pin through the spar kept in place with a cotter pin. The rest of the blade assembly was the same as the Pitcairn blade.

The same blade dampers were installed, the stainless steel trailing edge had the same slip joints, the same fittings were used to attach the droop cables which held the blades while they were not turning. The leading edge back to the spar was covered with preformed plywood and the entire blade covered with aircraft fabric. The rotor hub, universal blocks (which allowed flapping and lead and lag) and blade root end fittings were the same ones used on the light Pitcairn Autogiros; (PAA-1 and PA-18 series). These hubs and parts were supplied by Autogiros Specialties Company, a mechanical engineering firm which supplied all the early autogiro hubs and parts to Pitcairn, Kellett and Buhl.

The rotor pylon was a pioneer effort by Kellett which they improved and refined all through their models. It was basically a single large round tube with auxiliary light weight struts going aft to the rear of the cockpit. After a few early flights with the K-2, ¼" diameter, streamlined rods had to be added to brace the pylon to the upper longerons.

The powerplant was a Continental A-70 seven cylinder radial aircooled engine giving 165 hp at 2000 rpm. The weight of the engine was reported as "between 400 and 415 lbs."

Thrust was provided by a 9 foot 6 inch diameter propeller, either fixed-pitched metal or ground adjustable metal.

In reviewing the flight test reports of early K-2 Autogiros, problems of rotor roughness are mentioned. One complaint was referred to as "wind wobbles"—a kind of lateral vibration caused by improper rotor damper settings or improperly adjusted interblade cables.

Overheating of the Continental A-70 is mentioned during the early flights but seems to be corrected by reworking the cowling around the cylinders. One other thing that seemed to give problems was the rotor runup drive system. Broken ring gears and stripped pinion teeth are often mentioned. Because all these parts are common with the Pitcairn machines, no doubt Pitcairn had the same problems. But references, if any, were not available in research.

Balancing the Autogiro required much experimenting. The storage tank for the air starter was mounted in the tail to improve longitudinal balance. A lead weight was added inside the left-hand wing tip to improve the lateral balance. The pylon needed realigning to achieve proper

rotor axis angle fore and aft and laterally. Because the blades have a fixed angle to the flap and lead lag hinges (after rigging), the lateral and longitudinal adjustment of the pylon helps offset the unequal lift on the upwind side of the rotor and the downwind side. This effect was referred to as "mechanical feathering." The rotor blade on the right side (advancing) climbs, and the one on the left side (retreating) descends. This equalized the lift on right and left.

"CAA AIRCRAFT LISTING"
KELLETT K-2-A, 2 PO CLAg, 2-431

Engine	Continental R-670 210 hp
Fuel	35 gals. (One in fuselage 28 gals. and one in fuselage 7 gals.)
Oil	5 gals.
No. pass.	1
Baggage	25 lbs. (Pay load includes 32 lbs. for parachutes—40 lbs. less 8 lbs. for seat cushion removed.)
Standard wt	2265 lbs.
Spec. basis	Aero. Bulletin 7A, Section 3
Serial Nos.	1 to 12 eligible.

EQUIPMENT:(*Means net increase)

Class I: Battery (hot shot); Starter (Heywood) 29 lbs.

Low pressure tires; Propeller—fixed metal.
Class III: Nose skid 10 lbs.; Cockpit enclosure 19 lbs.; Propeller—adj. metal 16 lbs.*

Seven Kellett K-2 autogiro fuselages on the assembly line. The "landing gear" on the two at right are for mobility while assembling, not for flight.

(Smithsonian Photo)

K-2   (Kellett Photo)

Kellett K2 No. 2 cable rotor rigging can clearly be seen.
(Smithsonian Photo)

Kellett K2 built in 1932, held CAA approval. Engine Continental
R670 165 hp redesigned as K3 with Kinner C5 165 hp. About 24 of
the K2 and K3 were built during 1933 and 1934. (Kellett Photo)

Approved Type Certificate 437 was upgraded from "A" group 29 to ACT on July 17, 1931.

Specifications

Gross weight	*2265 lbs.
Empty weight	1556 lbs.
Useful load	*633 lbs.
Top speed	100 mph
Cruising speed	80 mph
Minimum speed	24 mph
Landing speed	0 mph

*Gross Weight figure is from CAA Spec. This would give a useful load of 609 lbs.
**Useful load is from Kellett's brochure

Price: Fly away Factor FAF $7,885
12 were manufactured

Standard equipment was: metal propeller, Heywood air starter, dual controls and compass. (A compass was not required by the CAA until about 1937.)

Four Kellett K2 autogiros.   (Dallin Photo)

Kellett K-3

Tokyo, 1932 —A ceremony for naming the two Kellett Autogiros recently purchased by the War Office with public contributions was held at the Yoyogi parade ground this morning in the presence of 20,000 people. Major-General Rensuke Isotani, on behalf of the War Minister, who is now in the Kwansai, read a message naming the planes the Aikkoku (patriotic) 81 and 82. The planes then made exhibition flights over the parade grounds.
(Kellett Photo)

The K-3 was an improvement on the K-2. The most significant change was the substitution of a Kinner C-5, 210 hp engine for the Continental A-70, 165 hp plant. The Kinner boasted 210 hp at 1900 rpm. The weight of the engine was reported "under 420 lbs." The low weight-to-horsepower ratio was somewhat in favor of the Kinner. The K-3 used an 8-foot 10-inch propeller.

Optional items were a "coupe' top" and a safety nose skid which protected the propeller in case of a noseup.

The horizontal tail plan form was changed for a more pleasing rounded shape on the elevators and stabilizer.

"CAA AIRCRAFT LISTING"
KELLETT K-3, 2 PO-CLAg, ATC 471

Engine	Kimmer C-5 210 hp
Fuel	35 gals.
Oil	5 gals.
No. pass.	1
Baggage	25 lbs. (Pay load includes 2 parachutes 20 lbs. each)
Standard wt.	2400 lbs.
Spec. basis	Approved Type Cert. No. 471

Serial Nos. 2,12,14 and up mfrd. prior to 9-30-39 eligible. Approval expired as of that date.

EQUIPMENT: (* Means net increase)
Class I: Battery (2 dry cell); Starter (Heywood): 7.50-10 tires; Adj. meter propeller.
Class III equipment: Cockpit enclosure 24 lbs.; Nose skid 10 lbs.

Approved Type Certificate 471 was granted March 26, 1932.

Specifications

Gross weight	2400 lbs.
Empty weight	1647 lbs.
Useful load	753 lbs.
Top speed	110 mph
Cruise speed	90 mph
Landing speed	15-20 mph
Rate of climb	980 ft./min. (SL)

Records indicate that six were built. Two K-2s were modified to K-3s. One went to the South Pole with Admiral Byrd. This was donated by the Pep Boys of auto parts stores fame. It was N 12615. Two were sold to Japan.

Standard equipment was: adjustable metal propeller, Heywood air starter, navigation lights and "Hotshot" (dry) battery.

First autogiro in the Argentine being inspected by army officers previous to first flights. The pilot is Edward E. Denniston of Philadelphia and the autogiro is a Kellett K-3 model manufactured in the United States by Kellett Autogiro Corporation. The navy officers are Captain Marco Zarr and Captain Mermos Hermosa and the scene is at Punta India Military Airport, Buenos Aires, Argentina.

(Kellett Photo)

Demonstration of the Kellett Autogiro at Palermo, Buenos Aires, Argentina. This was the first autogiro to be flown in the Argentine and created wide public interest. Mr. Leigh Wade, Kellett representative in the Argentine, is at the right, and pilot Edward E. Denniston at the left.

(Kellett Photo)

Kellett K-3 with "coupe top."

(Smithsonian Photo)

100

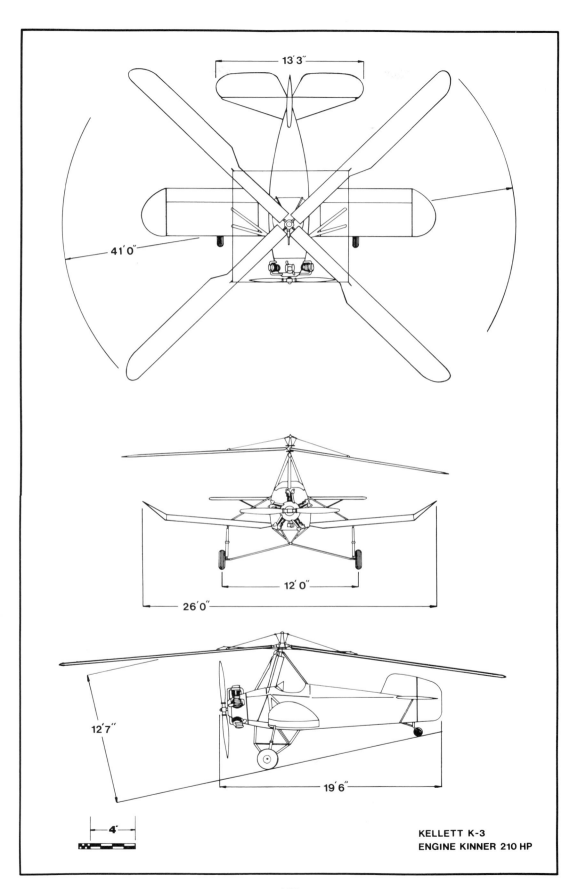

13'3"

41'0"

26'0"

12'0"

12'7"

19'6"

4'

KELLETT K-3
ENGINE KINNER 210 HP

Kellett K-3 autogiro with the Byrd Antarctic Expedition in 1933–1934. Bill McCormic, a Kellett test pilot was the pilot. Next to the autogiro the men are digging a "Pilgrim" airplane out of the snow. A mound of snow can be seen where another airplane is burned.

(Kellett Photo)

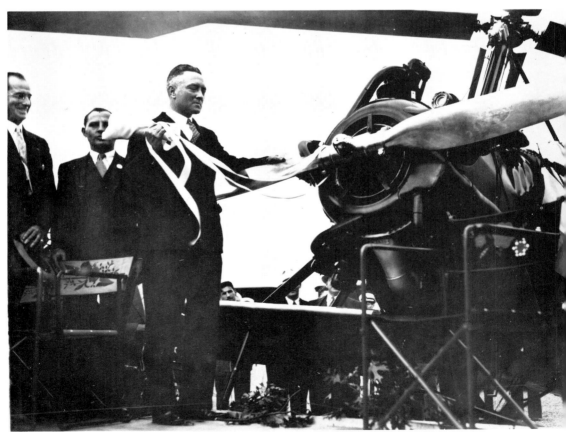

Admiral Richard E. Byrd christening the Kellett Autogiro, which accompanied his Antarctic Expedition at Central Airport, Camden, New Jersey in 1933.

(Kellett Photo)

Kellett Sky Ads

Another effort of Kellett Autogiro Co.: manufacturing, towing and leasing "Sky Ads."   (Wide World Photo)

In 1932 Kellett was featuring Sky Ads in addition to Autogiros. These were 9-foot high cloth letters made from red bunting and supported with bamboo poles. The letters could be readily assembled into words and messages and towed behind the autogiro. The combination had the double appeal of the autogiro and the Sky Ad.

Later messages were made up and leased to fixed wing operators for their use behind air planes. In 1937 Kellett sold the entire Sky Ad franchise to a local airport operator retaining only the patents.

Autogiro towing sky ad in August 1932. Hangars at old Philadelphia Municipal Airport at left.   (Kellett Photo)

Kellett K-4

Kellett K-4, last of the Kellett Autogiros with fixed wings. This was actually built from K-2 Serial No. 3. It was a mystery to the author why Kellett had gone back to the parallel-chord elevators in this model until it was discovered that this autogiro was actually K-2, serial 3. The K-3 series showed a more pleasing curved trailing edge. (Kellett Photo)

In 1933 Kellett announced a new model, the K-4. The most noticeable change was the absence of the familiar turned-up wing tips. A beautiful wing, tapered in plan and thickness had a single dihedral angle which put the tip at exactly the same place as the top of the turned-up tip. The landing gear, too, was somewhat simplified. The rotor pylon used the same large diameter forward member with only one aft member. But retaining the side braces as in the K-3. The appearance of the horizontal tail caused some confusion. When the K-3 was built, the horizontal tail had been redesigned to a rounded elevator. The K-4 showed the old K-2 square elevators. Actually the K-2, serial #3, was modified to make the K-4. A later Continental R-670 giving 210 hp was installed with a ground-adjustable Hamilton Standard aluminum propeller.

The fuselage, of course, coming from the K-2 serial #3, was gas welded steel tubes. The wing was wood with a plywood cover. The tail was wood with a fabric covering.

No price was announced. Only one was built. There is no record of a CAA approved Type Certificate being obtained. The autogiro was reported to have been sold to the Steel Pier in Atlantic City, New Jersey.

Specifications

Gross weight	2400 lbs.
Empty weight	1620 lbs.
Useful load	780 lbs.
Top speed	114 mph
Cruise speed	94 mph
Landing speed	not given
Rate of climb	940 ft./min.
Absolute ceiling	14,000 ft.
Service ceiling	12,500 ft.

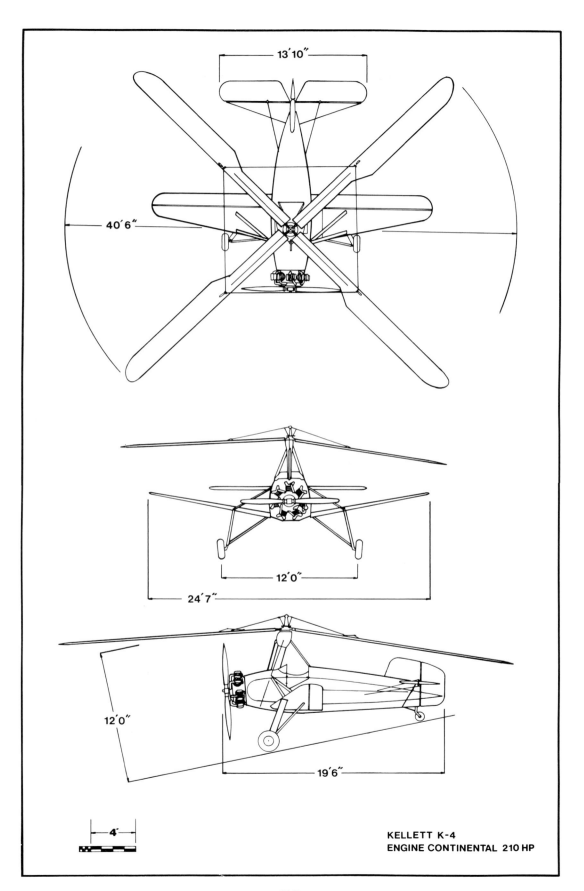

13′10″

40′6″

12′0″

24′7″

12′0″

19′6″

4′

KELLETT K-4
ENGINE CONTINENTAL 210 HP

105

The one and only Kellett K-4. No Department of Commerce certificate.

(Kellett Photo)

This head-on view shows the beautiful tapered wing. This Series Continental, originally 165 hp had been upgraded to 210 hp by this time. The tip of this wing was at the same point as the turned-up tip on K2-K3 models. It was said that this wing gave the same stability of the turned-up tips.

(Smithsonian Photo)

Kellett KD-1 (Army Air Corps YG-1)

Kellett YG-1B flying formation with a Republic P-36. Wallace Kellett was chairman of the board of Republic.   (Kellett Photo)

About 1935 Kellett announced a new model, the KD-1. The "D" denoted Direct Control. This meant that the control of the autogiro did not depend on airspeed for effectiveness.

As long as the rotor turned, control was adequate—even at zero airspeed. Control responses came from tilting the entire rotor head with the control stick in the direction that control was desired. This was similar to the Pitcairn PA-22, PA-35, PA-36, PA-34, PA-39 and XOP-2. Actually, Wallace Kellett and Chief Engineer Dick Prewitt went to Europe to see Cierva's C-30 Autogiro. The KD-1 was made more nearly a copy to that autogiro.

Several departures from earlier Kellett machines were noticeable. Seating was now tandem in open cockpits. The landing gear was nearly directly under the engine. The engine selected was a locally manufactured seven-cylinder radial air cooled Jacobs L4MA-7, developing 225 hp. The rear of the engine was especially modified to drive the rotor prior to takeoff using the engine starter pad.

Rotor blades were different from earlier Kellett blades. The chord was reduced to 12 inches from K-3, K-4's 23 inches. The airfoil section was a Göettingen 606. All other Kellett rotor airfoils had been nearly symmetrical while this one had nearly a flat underside. The upper curve was a high lift airfoil. Attachment of the ribs to the steel tube spar departed from the pinned-on method previously used in favor of the spot welded attachment used by Pitcairn. The ribs were routed from specially made 3-ply wood using vertical grain mahogany over horizontal grain birch. The mahogany layers were 1/16" thick and the birch 1/8". The trailing edge was spruce, the leading edge was ash. The entire blade was covered with 1/32" mahogany 3-ply, then covered with balloon cloth and doped to a smooth finish. The blades were balanced chordwise with a brass bar right at the nose and balanced spanwise by filling any of three boxes near the blade tip with lead shot as required.

The number of blades was reduced to three. The droop cables were eliminated by installing

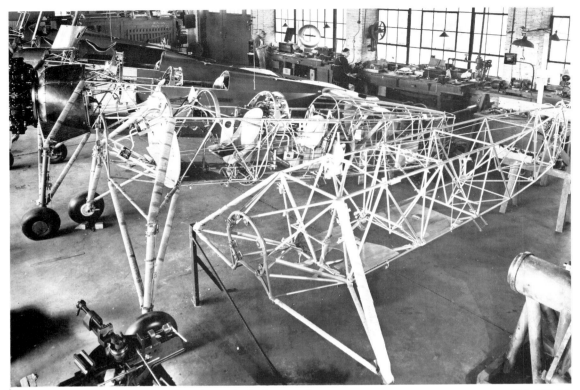

Kellett YG-1 Autogiro assembly line where six autogiro fuselages are shown. (Kellett Photo)

*Kellett blade shop showing blades in jigs. The right top side of blade frame next to right bottom side of blade being covered with 1/32"
plywood. When both sides were covered with plywood they were then covered with cotton fabric and doped. These are KD-1/YG-1
blades.*
(Kellett Photo)

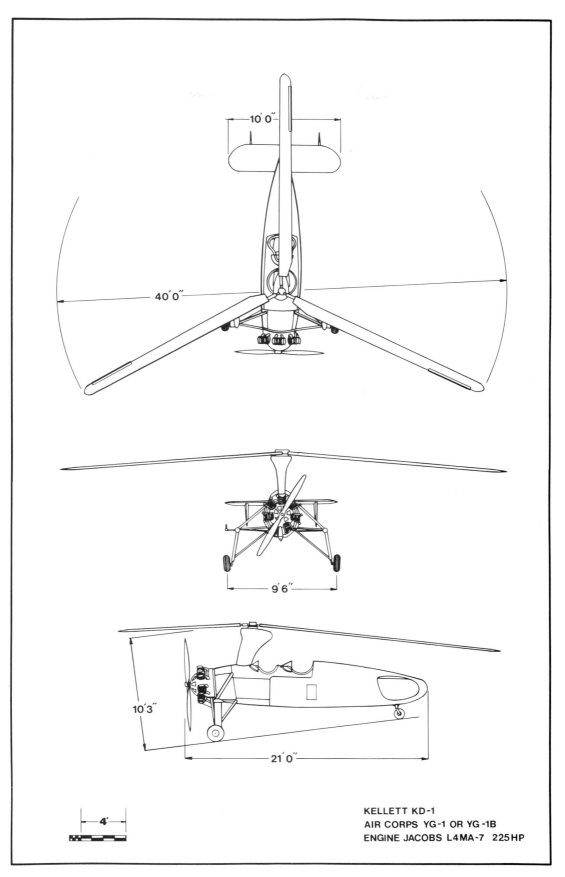

10' 0"

40' 0"

9' 6"

10' 3"

21' 0"

4'

KELLETT KD-1
AIR CORPS YG-1 OR YG-1B
ENGINE JACOBS L4MA-7 225HP

Part of Kellett YG-1 assembly line. One autogiro is nearly complete. (Kellett Photo)

Kellett YG-1 Autogiro assembly line of five autogiros. (Kellett Photo)

Kellett's KD-1 prototype in 1952 after being "rescued" by the author with a very large assist from the American Legion Pilots Post at the request of Wallace Kellett, Kellett's president. It was to be restored but Wallace Kellett's untimely death put an end to that project.

(Kellett Photo)

droop stops at the hub. Blade dampers now inside the spar working on a cam at the hub kept the blades spaced equally from each other. As the blades tried to lead or lag the damper came into play returning the blade to the proper spacing. The rotor hub was neat and simple. The runup gears were now inside a housing containing oil for lubrication.

The rotor support was simple in design. Only one large, round, heat-treated steel tube carried the flight loads to the fuselage. A streamlined aluminum fairing housed the support or pylon tube as well as the vertical drive shaft. At the bottom of the shaft within the cowl, a rotor brake was provided to stop the rotor after landing. The rest of the rotor spinup system consisted of a power takeoff housing on the back of the engine. A leather-lined cone clutch permitted the engine to be engaged slowly and smoothly and quickly disengaged before takeoff. The horizontal shaft passed through the firewall to an intermediate gearbox where the drive angle was changed from horizontal to vertical. On the output side of this box was an overrunning clutch to permit the rotor to turn if the engine clutch

should fail to disengage on takeoff. A torque-limiting shear pin fastened the vertical shaft to the gear box. The pin would shear if excess torque was applied to the rotor on runup. If the pin should fail when the rotor was near takeoff rpm, a takeoff could still be made. The rotor rpm would increase on the takeoff run. A pin could be easily replaced when back on the ground.

The fuselage was built up of gas welded steel tubing heavily faired with light weight aluminum bows and longitudinal members. The forward part was covered with sheet aluminum. The fuel tanks formed the fairing and covering for the sides of the fuselage at the front cockpit. The rest of the fuselage was fabric covered.

The horizontal tail was assembled from solid spruce spars with built-up ribs with cap strips and plywood webs. The stabilizers were internally braced with steel rods. The leading edge was made from a round steel tube and covered with plywood from the leading edge to the front spar, top and bottom. The tip and trailing edge was formed from a round steel tube that was gradually formed into a streamline shape as it left the rear spar. A handhold was provided in the tip aft of the front spar for ground handling.

The rudder and vertical tail surfaces were welded steel tube assemblies. All surfaces were fabric covered and doped.

The landing gear was a wide tread type with Bendix air and oil shock struts. The tires were 8:00 x 15 with 6 inch Hayes Industries mechanical brakes. The tail wheel was a 10 inch with a swivel device that could be locked in the steerable position. The tail shock strut was an air-oil type. The rest of the tail group consisted of a small rudder carrying the fuselage side shape to a rounded ending. The horizontal tail was ground-adjustable. The left side was installed with the airfoil in its normal upright position while the right hand side had the airfoil inverted. This imparted a twist to the fuselage which directly opposed the propeller torque. As power was applied and the air stream from the propeller increased, the right side wanted to "lift down" while the left lifted in the "up" position. When the power and air stream was reduced, the lift reduced. The adjustment also permitted various angles of incidence to be selected. They could be used to compensate for c.g changes to the autogiro through its life as well as to compensate for propeller torque. Because the rotor was not driven in flight, there was no rotor torque transmitted to the fuselage. Two vertical fixed surfaces were attached to the bottom of the horizontal stabilizers where there was no risk of their being struck by the rotor. The horizontal stabilizers were supported by two aluminum streamlined struts on either side extending down to the bottom longerons.

Cockpit controls were the same as those found in any open cockpit airplane with certain additions. The rear cockpit control stick was provided with a stick lock where the stick was placed when the rotor was at rest or below approximately 100 rpm. The stick was pushed forward into the lock soon after landing and was kept in the lock while starting the rotor until about 100 rpm was reached (flight rotor rpm was 210). There was no danger of getting the stick into the lock in flight because the lock was at the extreme forward end of the stick travel.

A clutch lever was located just under the throttle on the left side of the cockpit so that no time was lost in getting the throttle wide open when the clutch was released.

Rudder pedals were used to steer the tail wheel while on the ground. In flight the pedals would aid in making a tighter turn although they were not needed for a normal turn. When the

stick is rolled either way and the autogiro banked, it would turn in that direction. Rolling out of a turn could be done in the same way without adverse yaw.

The KD-1 controlled easily with an extremely light touch and was quite sensitive. Longitudinal and lateral bungees were provided to relieve control loads caused by an unbalanced autogiro. The pilot occupied the rear seat and the observer or passenger sat up front. The rear cockpit had an altimeter, airspeed indicator tachometers for engine and rotor, compass, oil temperature and oil pressure gauges. Glass sight gauges on the rear side of the fuel tanks provided fuel quantity information. These could only be seen from the rear cockpit.

A Jacobs L4MB7 delivered 225 hp through a fixed-pitch Curtiss-Reed propeller. A Heywood air starter cranked the engine. CAA Certification was obtained. Only one KD-1 was built.

Specifications

Gross weight	2250 lbs.
Empty weight	1315 lbs.
Useful load	935 lbs.
Fuel	44 gal. (in two tanks)
Oil	4 gal.
Performance not available	

Prototype Kellett KD-1 taking off from the street in Washington, D.C. *(Kellett Photo)*

Head-on view of Kellett KD-1 prototype with blades unfolded. (Kellett Photo)

Kellett YG-1 with blades folded for taxiing, towing or storing. Unfolding time is only five minutes. (Kellett Photo)

The Kellett staff in front of the factory in Philadelphia. Not many can now be identified. Top row: (left to right) Hugh Mulvey, Engineer; Arnold Rasmussen, Mechanic; (three unknown) Wallace Kellett; Dick Prewett, Chief Engineer; (two unknown) Lew Levitt, Test Pilot; (unknown) Haig Kurjian, Engineer; (two unknown) Rod Kellett. Front row: Mark DuPont, Mechanic; (unknown) Jack Schwartz, Mechanic; (the rest of the front row is unidentified). 1934–35 KD-1 prototype autogiro is in background. (Kellett Photo)

At the same time that the KD-1 was announced, Kellett moved from Philadelphia's Municipal Airport which was frequently flooded by the nearby Delaware River. The move was to a 30,000 square foot building about a mile away on Island Road.

After the retirement of the prototype KD-1 about 1943, it rested many years in the basement storage area of Philadelphia's Commercial Museum. It was rescued in 1953 by the author at the request of Wallace Kellett who had a desire to restore it for exhibition. Unfortunately, Mr. Kellett had an untimely death before the restoration was begun. Kellett management had no interest in the project. It was stored, along with many famous cousins, in a barn on Harold Pitcairn's estate. In 1959 a fire destroyed the barn and all the autogiros including the KD-1. Some of its parts were saved and put into a reborn KD-1 bearing serial number 101 in 1959. Kellett extensively demonstrated the "new" KD-1 in 1960, planning to go into production again.

"C.A.A. AIRCRAFT LISTING"
KELLETT KD-1, KD-1A, KD-1B, TC 712

I—SPECIFICATIONS PERTINENT
   TO ALL MODELS:

Spec. Basis   Type Certificate No. 712
              (Aero, Bulletin 7A requirements)

EQUIPMENT: (Datum is center line of station 1L (lower engine mount attachment to fuselage) (*Means net increase)

Class I:

101. Propeller—fixed metal   54 lbs. (-50)
     (a) Curtiss-Reed 55501 (For KD-1 and KD-1B)
     (b) Curtiss-Reed 55501-5 (for KD-1A)

102. 7.00-5 wheels (Hayes) with brakes and tires   33 lbs. (-20)

103. 10.5 in. streamline tail wheel (Bendix B) and tire   6 lbs. (+172)

104. Starter
     (a) (Heywood) (For KD-1) 32 lbs.(−18)
     (b) (Eclipes E-80) (For KD-1A and KD-1B)   18 lbs. (−19)

105. Battery—12 volt (Reading) and box 31 lbs.   (−5)

106. Generator
     (a) 15 amp. (Eclipse LV-180)
     (for KD-1 and KD 1B)   15 lbs. (−21)

(b) 15 amp. (Leece-Neville D-3)
(for KD-1A)   16 lbs. (−21)
Class II:
200. Misc. items as noted in approved weight and balance report.
Class III:
301. Flexible pylon installation   10 lbs.
302. Radio (Model KD-1A only) 40 lbs. (+2)

NOTE A. Each aircraft manufactured after Jan. 14, 1941 must, prior to original certification, satisfactorily pass:

(a) An inspection for workmanship, materials and conformity before any covering, metal priming or final finish is applied.
(b) A Final inspection of the completed aircraft.
(c) A check of flight characteristics.

NOTE 1. Eligible for export as follows subject to inspection for equipment specified in Chapter XII of Inspection Handbook: (April 4, 1941)

a) Canada—Landplane. Skiplane—not eligible
(b) All other countries except Australia, Great Britain and New Zealand.

NOTE 2. Prior to original certification, the firewall of Model KD-1A aircraft must be brought up to current requirements. Facing forward side of existing firewall with 1/8 in. asbestos firmly secured and finished with oil and moisture-proof pain will be considered the equivalent of current requirements.

NOTE 3. Placard front cockpit is Model KD-1A, "Solo flying from rear seat only."

II—MODEL KD-1 DESIGNATION 2 POLAg:

Engine	Jacobs L-4MA
Placard limits	Maximum, except takeoff —in. Hg., 2000rpm (225 hp) Takeoff (1 minute) —in. Hg., 2200 rpm (245 hp)
Propeller	Maximum permissible diameter 106 in.
Placard speed	Never exceed 126 mph True Ind.
Fuel capacity	48 gals. (Two fuselage tanks at 24 gals. each) (+24)
Oil capacity	4 gals. (−8)
No. passengers	1 (+31), pilot at (+66)
Baggage	30 lbs. (+86)
Standard wt.	2250 lbs.
C.G. limits	(+9.2) and (+13.8)
Serial Nos.	101 and up eligible per NOTE A

III—MODEL KD 1-A DESIGNATION 2 POLAg: (Same as U.S. Army Air Corps Model G-1B)

Engine	Jacobs L-4-MA7
Placard limits	Maximum, except takeoff —in. Hg., 2000 rpm (225 hp) Takeoff (one minute) —in. Hg., 2200 rpm (245 hp)
Propeller	Maximum permissible diameter 106 in.
Placard speed	Never exceed 126 mph True Ind.
Fuel capacity	30 gals. (Two fuselage tanks at 15 gals. each) (+17)
Oil capacity	4 gals. (−8)
No. passengers	1 (+31) or (+66) (See NOTE 3)
Baggage	30 lbs. (+86)
Standard wt.	2400 lbs.
C.G. limits	(+9.2) and (+14.4)
Serial Nos.	101 to 106, inclusive, and 108 eligible per NOTES A and 2

IV—MODEL KD-1B DESIGNATION 1 PCLAg
(Same as KD-1 except desig., std. weight and minor structural changes)

Engine	Jacobs L-4MA
Placard limits	Maximum, except takeoff —in. Hg., 2000rpm (225 hp) Takeoff (one minute) —in. Hg., 2200 rpm (245 hp)
Propeller	Maximum permissible diameter 106 in.
Placard speed	Never exceed 126 mph True Ind.
Fuel capacity	30 gals. (Two fuselage tanks at 15 gals. each (+17)
Oil Capacity	4 gals (−8)
No. passengers	None
Baggage	300 lbs. (Front pit) (+18) 20 lbs. (Aft of pilot) (+95)
Standard wt.	2400 lbs.
C.G. limits	(+9.8) and (+14.4)
Serial Nos.	101 and up eligible per NOTE A

Kellett KD-1 prototype. Compare the somewhat crude sheet metal work to later copies of the KD-1.   (Kellett Photo)

Kellett KD-1. Lou Leavitt delivering bag of mail on Philadelphia's Thirtieth Street post office roof. This was a demonstration before the Eastern Air Lines scheduled service.   (Kellett Photo)

Kellett YG-1 Autogiros at the U.S. Air Force Flight Training School, Wright Field, Dayton, Ohio, about 1938. This was the first rotary wing aircraft flight school initiated by the U.S. Air Force. (Developed for U.S. Air Force under contract with U.S. Air Force.)

(Kellett Photo)

Kellett YG-1A with its army decorations. The fuel tanks are on each side at the front cockpit. The right hand horizontal stabilizer had an inverted airfoil while the left was conventional to impart a rolling moment in proportion to the prop wash and torque imput.

(Bond Brothers/Kellett Photo)

First autogiro class at the completion of graduation review, May 21, 1938, Patterson Field, Dayton, Ohio. The officer in civilian clothes is General Robins, Commanding Officer of Wright-Patterson Field, Col. Gregory (2nd from left).

(Kellett Photo)

Kellett KD-1A

The author, assistant project engineer and experimental test pilot with Bob Kenworthy the project engineer for Kellett 1958–1960, congratulating each other on the first flight of "Reborn" KD-1A. (Kellett Photo)

The KD-1A was a slightly modified KD-1. An engine driven generator and an electric engine starter were added. The fuel tankage was reduced from 44 to 30 gallons. Seven of these were sold to the U.S. Army Air Corps as Model YG-1B.

They were stationed at Ft. Bragg to train pilots as artillery spotters and to carry out other liaison missions. On one occasion a pilot talked over a telephone line that had been dropped to the ground through an Army switchboard to a general in his office.

Two were bailed back to Kellett for developmental work. One was designated the XR-2 and the other XR-3 (see later chapters). The remaining five were given to the border patrol for Texas/Mexico border surveillance. They were declared surplus and drifted around Texas and Arizona. One found its way to Canada where Atlas Aviation wanted to use it for towing advertising banners. The author "taught" their pilot to fly it by telephone, and he made a successful solo flight. It was sold to the Leavans Brothers of Canada and, while in their possession, it was destroyed by fire following a takeoff accident.

In 1960 Kellett found one of the YG-1B's and two engines in Phoenix, Arizona. They bought them for parts to use as backup for the KD-1A that they were demonstrating.

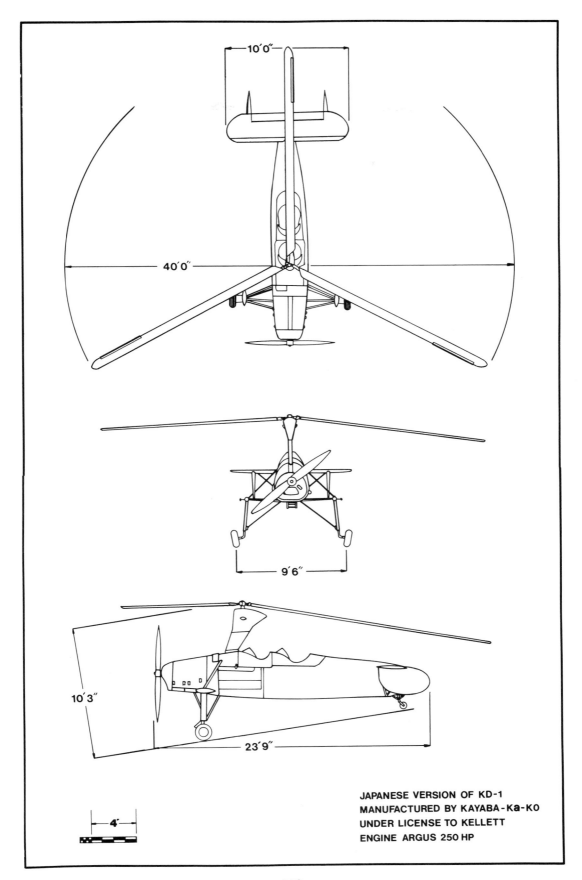

10'0"

40'0"

9'6"

10'3"

23'9"

4'

JAPANESE VERSION OF KD-1
MANUFACTURED BY KAYABA-Ka-KO
UNDER LICENSE TO KELLETT
ENGINE ARGUS 250 HP

Rotor head of Kellett KD-1A autogiro. The head tilts fore and aft and left or right with pilot's control stick for lateral and longitudinal control. *(Howard Levy Photo)*

Rear (pilot's) cockpit in the Kellett KD-1A, 1958–59. *(Howard Levy Photo)*

Kellett KD-1A with blades folded, 1958–59. *(Howard Levy Photo)*

Kellett KD-1A being put in a barn with rotor blades folded, 1958–59. *(Howard Levy Photo)*

A Kellett KD-1A built in 1959 to create interest in the autogiro. It was made from the XR-3 parts of the original KD-1 and parts of the KD-1B. New rotor blades were made at this time. Roland "Blackie" Maier, pilot.   *(Howard Levy Photo)*

Successful forced landing Kellett YG-1B Wingless Autogiro, while engaged in U.S.-Mexico Border PAtrol. Operated by U.S. Immigration Service, 1941.   *(Kellett Photo)*

Kellett KD-1B

The former Eastern Airlines Kellett Autogiro in 1959 while in the author's possession. Note all E.A. identity has been removed.

(G. Townson Photo)

In 1939 the Post Office Department advertised for bids to fly airmail by autogiro from Philadelphia's 30th Street Post Office roof to Camden, New Jersey's Central Airport. The Post Office roof was ten stories high and about a city block square.

Eastern Airlines was the successful bidder at $3.86 per mile. The distance was 6 miles. Five round trips a day were flown six days a week.

Kellett was selected as the builder of the autogiro which was basically the same as the KD-1A except that a mail pit replaced the front cockpit. An enclosure covered the rear cockpit. All details of construction were the same as the KD-1A. A very high percentage of scheduled flights were completed. The pilot was Kellett's test pilot, John M. Miller. By act of Congress, all civil air regulations were waived and the operation left to Miller's discretion. The first scheduled flight was July 5, 1939 and the last flight, July 4, 1940. Three hundred pounds of mail could be carried per flight.

The KD-1B was granted a Standard CAA Approved Type Certificate under ATC 712. Specifications and performance were almost the same as the KD-1A.

Gross weight	2400 lbs.
Empty weight	1600 lbs.
Useful load	800 lbs.

Performance (guaranteed)	100 mph
Landing speed	20 mph
Initial rate of climb	800 ft./min.

In addition to the usual instruments, the KD-1B had: directional Giro, artificial horizon, rate of climb indicator, turn and bank indicator, clock, 15-watt transmitter, three-band receiver, fire extinguisher, and a first aid kit.

The only accident in the year's operation was when the autogiro rolled on its side on the roof in very gusty air. It had operated in winds as high as 50 mph. It was not possible to get the autogiro down off the roof for repairs, so it was repaired and test flown from the roof ten stories high. The flying was shared by Paul (Skip) Lukins, one of Pitcairn's flight instructors and autogiro test pilot. Skip was in the KD-1B when it upset on the Post Office.

At least one passenger was carried to the roof in the autogiro. Jose Uturbi, popular pianist, was flown on one occasion with special permission of the CAA. Only one KD-1B was built. Eastern sold it about December of 1941. It found its way into the author's hands in 1953, after a minor ground accident. The blades and part of the spinup mechanism were damaged. After repair with Kellett's technical help, it was sold to them. They planned to use it as a research aircraft for high speed flight studies. It was des-

Eastern Airlines Captain John Miller on final approach for Philadelphia, Pennsylvania's Thirtieth Street post office roof. The autogiro is a Kellett KD-1B. (Kellett Photo)

Kellett KD-1B Autogiro which was operated from June 1939 to June 1940 in daily air mail shuttle service between the roof of the Post Office, Philadelphia, Pennsylvania and the Camden, New Jersey Municipal Airport. This aircraft made five round trips daily carrying all United States Air Mail to and from the city of Philadelphia. During its year of operation, the Kellett Autogiro completed more than 90% of all scheduled flights. More than 2,300 takeoffs and landings from the Post Office roof were made. (Kellett Photo)

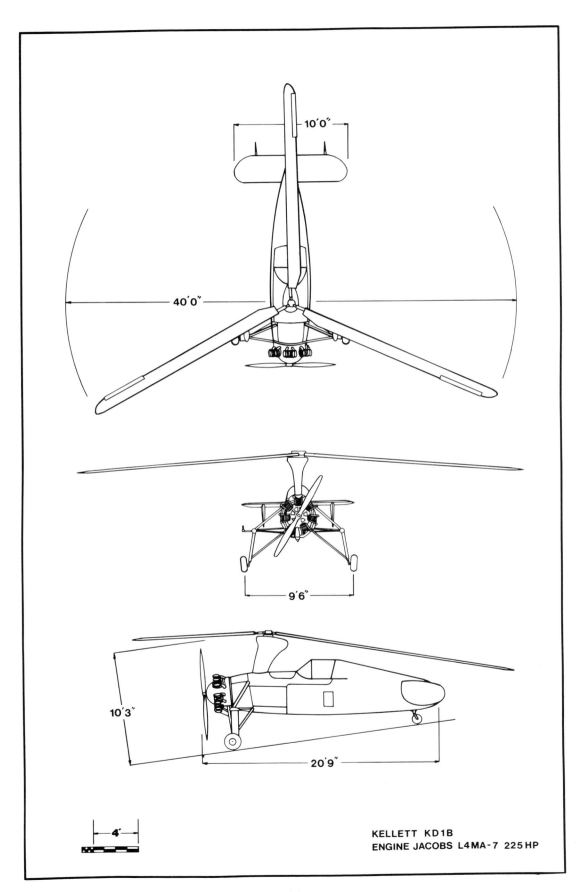

10′0″

40′0″

9′6″

10′3″

20′9″

4′

KELLETT KD1B
ENGINE JACOBS L4MA-7 225 HP

124

Kellett KD-1B Autogiro used to carry mail from Philadelphia's Thirtieth Street Post Office to Central Airport in adjoining Camden, New Jersey. Captain John Miller, Eastern Airlines' Autogiro pilot. (Kellett Photo)

Loading mail in Eastern Airlines' KD-1B Autogiro at Camden, New Jersey for a trip to the roof of Philadelphia's Thirtieth Street Post Office. (Kellett Photo)

Captain John Miller preparing to take Eastern Airlines' Kellett KD-1B Autogiro for a flight to nearby Camden, New Jersey Central Airport. Notice the "miniature" fuel truck (just beyond the onlookers) for fueling the autogiro. (International News Photo)

ignated the KH-17 with a 300 hp Jacobs R-755 engine in the nose. It also had two additional 150 hp Lycoming engines with the propellers turning in opposite directions mounted in stub wings on either side of the fuselage. It was flown once or twice with only the center engine and without the wings. The project was abandoned because of high control stick forces. The rotor blades used were the front rotor blades from a Piasecke HUP helicopter which was a tandem rotor helicopter. A feathering rotor control system was used instead of the KD-1 type tilting head.

Kellett YO-60

Kellett YO-60 with Kellett's chief test pilot, Dave Driscoll (L). Other persons in photo not identified. (Kellett Photo)

The Army Air Corps liked the YG-1B but needed more power and more useful load. Above all, they wanted vertical takeoff. This was 1940 and the helicopter was not yet available. Although the Air Corps had a helicopter under construction, its usefulness was yet some time away.

The proposed XO-60 (Kellett did not assign their own model number to the YO-60) it was a growth version of the KD-1A.

The rotor system was similar to the KD-1A, using the same type blades and familiar construction. A heat-treated 4130 steel tube was the main member, with plywood ribs and 1/32" plywood cover. Some YO-60s were flown with slightly different blades with tapered thickness and plan. These had step tapered spars and were fabric covered instead of 1/32" plywood covered. The leading edge back to the spar tube was plywood covered.

The rotor system was different with the addition of the hardware necessary for jump takeoff. The blades were set at "no lift" angle for runup. The rotor was speeded up to 280-290 rpm about 80 or 90 more than the cruise rpm. When the clutch was released a counterweight on each

blade twisted the blade upward to about 8 degrees. Then, as the rpm bled off, the angle came back to 3 degrees. At this time, the autogiro should be at about 10 feet altitude. Relieved of its rotor load, the engine came up to takeoff rpm and flew the YO-60 off the top of the jump.

There was one problem of jumping a tail sitting autogiro. Because the tail was down, the rotor was tilting slightly aft. When the takeoff did take place, the aircraft actually jumped backwards and the propeller had to overcome the little bit of backward inertia before forward thrust could take effect.

The same rotor arrangement as YG-1 series was retained, but the motion dampers that were inside the blade spars as in the KD-1/YG-1 had to be assisted by dampers attached from blade to blade near the root end.

The power takeoff for the rotor spinup was improved. There had been many problems with the leather faced clutch on earlier models. The clutch would either slip and chatter or fail to release completely. When the shear pin in the vertical shaft did not shear as it was supposed to, damage could be done to the drive shaft.

126

Kellett YO-60   *(Kellett Photo)*

Kellett YO-60 damaged in a ground accident. The autogiro was being run up with the control stick in the lock (forward) position where it is left until takeoff is about to commence. The YO-60 was capable of making a "jump takeoff." The pilot accidentally tripped the jump control and the autogiro jumped, nosing over with the stick locked forward. This autogiro is restored for exhibit and is in the National Air Museum.   *(Kellett Photo)*

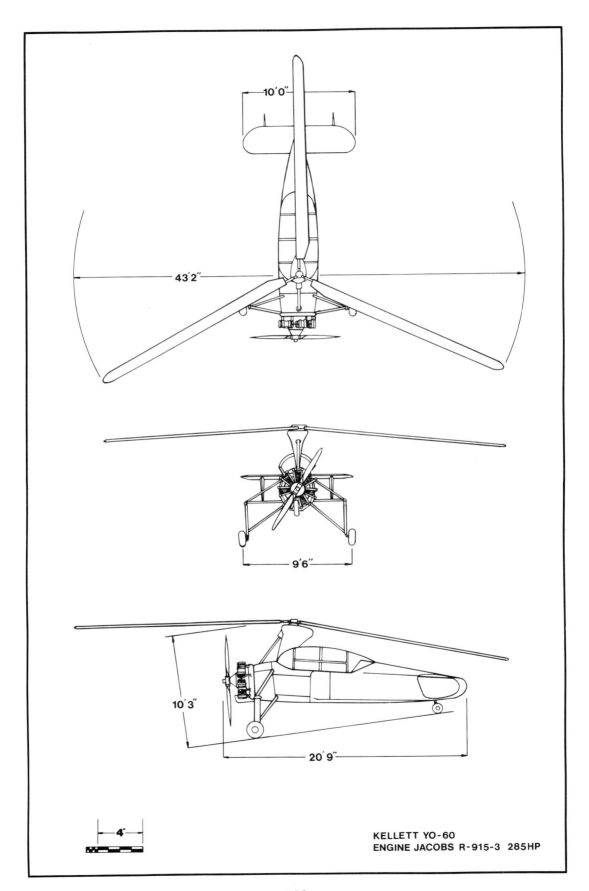

10'0"

43'2"

9'6"

10'3"

20'9"

4'

KELLETT YO-60
ENGINE JACOBS R-915-3 285HP

128

COL Frank Gregory, Dave Driscoll (Kellett test pilot) and Wallace Kellett in 1942 with a Kellett YO-60 autogiro at Philadelphia International Airport near Kellett's plant.
(Kellett Photo)

COL Frank Gregory with chief engineer Dick Prewitt at the Kellett Factory, 1942.
(Kellett Photo)

The new style clutch had discs and used a planetary reduction gear system at the engine with a larger drive shaft running directly from the power takeoff on the engine to the rotor head.

One of the major changes put the pilot in the front seat and added a transparent plastic cover over both cockpits and a large transparent plastic panel in the belly beneath the pilot's feet. The observer's seat could swivel so he could ride backwards and work at a small table behind the rear seat. When the observer was not in place, balast had to be carried in the rear cockpit.

The long-travel Bendix shock struts were mounted nearly-vertical. The entire landing gear could be removed including the outrigger struts thus reducing the width of the fuselage for shipping from more than 8 feet to the width of the fuselage.

The engine mount, too, was removable at the firewall. In this way a quick change powerplant package could be stocked.

The fuselage structure was similar to the earlier KD-1/YG-1. The fairing was different

1942 ARMY NEWCOMER—This was the first photograph to be released of the U.S. Army Air Force new YO-60 autogiro, produced by Kellett Aircraft Corporation, Philadelphia, Pennsylvania, builders of earlier giro types for the army. Kellett has completed delivery of a service test lot of these aircraft, which are being operated for tactical studies and instructional work. Note the huge bubble-type canopy which provides excellent vision for the crew of the ship. Powered by a Jacobs 300 horsepower engine, this member of the 15-year-old line of Kellett rotary-wing craft possessed maneuverability characteristics which were improved by design innovations and increased power.

(Kellett Aircraft Photo)

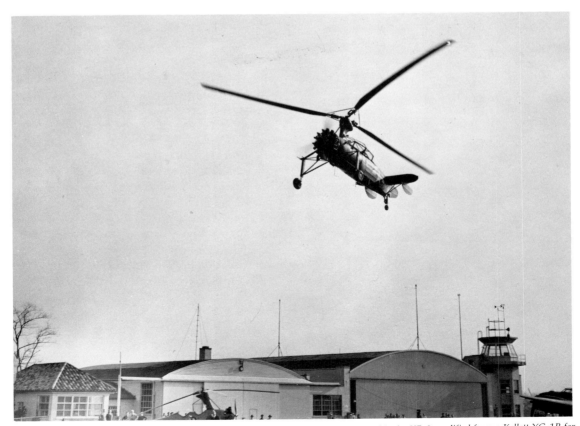

Kellett YO-6O autogiro landing at DuPont Field Wilmington, Delaware. On the ground is the XR-3 modified from a Kellett YG-1B for research work.

(Kellett Photo)

The last Kellett Autogiro YO-60 with the KD-1 prototype.

(Kellett Photo)

with flatter sides giving the observer better downward vision out the side windows. The enclosure over the two cockpits hinged open and slid to the right to permit entrance and exit from the cockpits on the left.

The powerplant was a Jacobs R-915-3, seven cylinder, aircooled, radial engine providing 330 hp through a Hamilton-Standard constant speed propeller.

The model was soon changed from XO-60 to YO-60 and seven were built. Only six were delivered, one was damaged in a runup accident and was not repaired. The National Air Museum in Washington has restored this autogiro for exhibit and it can be seen there along with the helicopters.

Specifications

Gross weight	2640 lbs.
Empty weight	
Useful Load	
Top speed	122mph
Cruise speed	
Landing speed	

Kellett XR-2

Kellett XR-2, one of the YG-1B autogiros with an experimental landing gear and constant speed propeller. It was destroyed in a runup accident and it never flew.   *(Kellett Photo)*

Kellett did not give their model numbers to XR-2 or XR-3. These were the only two "non helicopters" to get XR designations by the military. The XR-1 was the Platt-LePage helicopter and the XR-4 was a Sikorsky helicopter. Earlier the autogiro had "O" designations for the Navy as "XOP-1" and XOP-2." "P" was for Pitcairn. The Army Air Corps had no such manufacturer designators. YG-1 (A&B) were Kellett Autogiros. The YG-2 was the Army Air Corps version of Pitcairn's Navy XOP-2. Later the Army Air Corps designated all observation craft, either

fixed or rotorwing as "O" of "XO." "XO" indicated Experimental Observation. "YO" indicated a service test model. When the model was accepted, the "Y" was dropped. The autogiro never made it to this level because the helicopter took its place with the military. YO-60 was Kellett's machine, while the XO-61 was Pitcairn's.

The XR-2 was modified YG-1B with a jump takeoff system the same as the XO-60 and with a 330 hp Jacobs engine installed. It used a single beam landing gear instead of the outriggers, etc. A Hamilton-Standard constant-speed propeller replaced the Curtiss-Reed.

The XR-2 never flew. It was totally destroyed in a ground runup accident.

Specifications

Gross weight	2400 lbs.
Empty weight	
Useful load	
Top Speed	106 mph *
Cruise speed	
Landing speed	

*Never flown

Kellett XR-2 without blades. (Note landing gear.) (Kellett Photo)

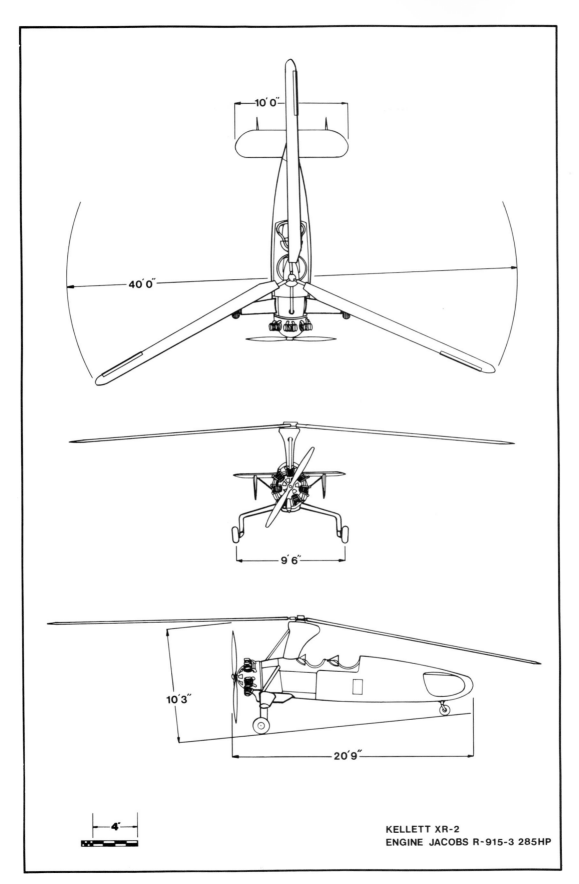

10' 0"

40' 0"

9' 6"

10' 3"

20' 9"

4"

KELLETT XR-2
ENGINE JACOBS R-915-3 285HP

133

Kellett XR-3

Kellett XR-3 rebuilt from YG-1B as test bed for cyclic rotor control system. Blades to be used on the XR-8 helicopter were said to be tested on this craft.   *(Kellett Photo)*

The XR-3 was used as a flying test bed for rotor blades and components to be used on Kellett's XR-8 helicopter that was being designed.

In general it had the same dimensions as the YG-1B using the fuselage, tail and landing gear with no changes. The only change to the power-plant was the use of the YO-60 power takeoff. As in the YO-60, the intermediate gear box was eliminated driving from the back of the engine to a modified YO-60 rotor head.

The head was locked so that it did not tilt. Control, instead, was done by feathering the blades cyclically as is done now in a helicopter. Jump takeoff was provided by manually operated "collective" pitch control of the blade pitch angle for takeoff and a quicker descent. The normal blade for the XR-3 was tapered in thickness and plan form. Plywood ribs were spot welded through their metal collars to the heat-treated 4130 steel spar tube. Plywood covered the leading edge of the blade then the blade was fabric covered and doped. Because of the extra weight of the hub controls and blade controls, blade-to-blade dampers had to be added.

Specifications

Gross weight	2640 lbs.
Empty weight	
Useful load	
Top speed	106 mph
Cruise speed	
Landing speed	

The rotor pylon was mounted on rubber at the fuselage to eliminate vibration. This was later blocked out and extra struts were added to the pylon to brace it.

A movie camera was mounted on the top of the rotor head, rotating with the blade that could take pictures of one blade that was going to be used on the XR-8 helicopter. The blades were flown, photographed and studied while the autogiro was flown in various modes of flight. When pilots saw the pictures of the wild gyrations the blades went through—bending, flapping and twisting— they almost quit flying the autogiro.

Pilots who flew the XR-3 like it very much. One takeoff was made with the autogiro buried

Kellett XR-3 Autogiro, one on the YG-1B autogiros with a cyclically controlled rotor instead of a tilting head add jump takeoff ability. (Kellett Photo)

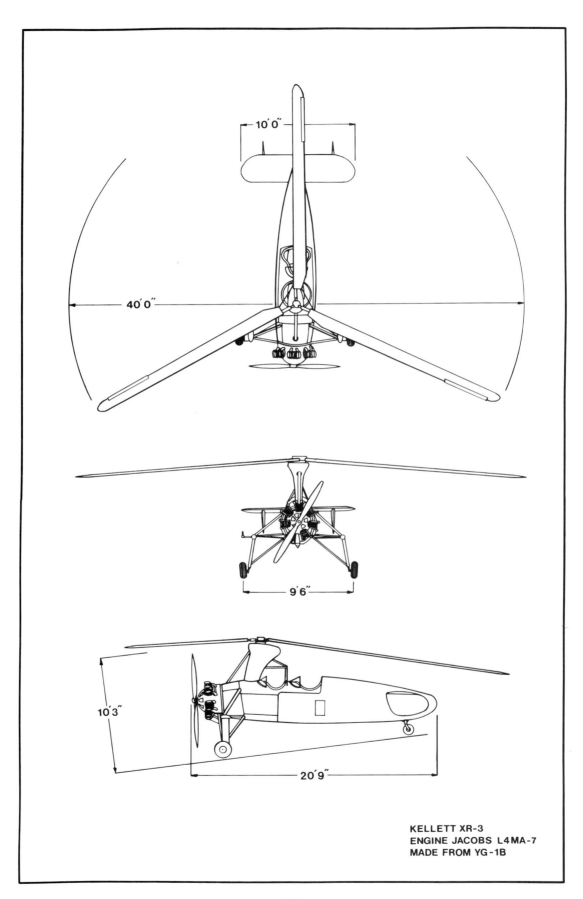

10′ 0″

40′ 0″

9′ 6″

10′ 3″

20′ 9″

KELLETT XR-3
ENGINE JACOBS L4MA-7
MADE FROM YG-1B

FIGURE NO. 2.

Kellett XR-3 rotor head showing movie camera mount on top of hub and comutator ring for electrical control of the camera. Camera followed one blade as it rotated. (Kellett Photo)

Another view of XR-3 autogiro. (Kellett Photo)

FIGURE NO. 6

Close view of comutator ring that permitted electrical control of the camera while it was rotating. (Kellett Photo)

Camera case. Note camera lense pointing down one blade. Comutator ring can be seen below rotor. (Kellett Photo)

in a snowdrift higher than its wheels. The autogiro jumped straight up without any forward motion.

At the end of its tests, it was sold surplus to Westinghouse who had an aerodynamic research center in Schenectady, New York.

After the YO-61, all autogiro building ceased. There was some activity in Canada where a light autogiro called an "Avion" was built. It never went to production. A United States fertilizer producer backed a two-place tandem-seat pusher. It was certificated and a few aircraft were produced. A company called Skyways Engineering in Indiana became an autogiro licensee in the fifties. They planned to produce the old Pitcairn AC-35 design. They could no longer get the PopJoy engine used in the AC-35, so the autogiro did not fly as well. They abandoned the project.

In 1959, Kellett Aircraft Corporation demonstrated a KD-1A which they had assembled from the remains of their XR-3, the KD-1B and some new parts. There was talk of firm orders and plans for production, but it all was dropped in 1960. McCulloch Motors of Los Angeles, the chain saw people, certified a two-place pusher using the front rotor from their MC-4 helicopter. About 100 were sold from their Havasu City plant before they dropped it. Since 1974 or so, there has been no serious activity. Igor Benson has continued to market the most successful autogiro type under the name, Gyrocopter.

The author (standing) congratulating Roland "Blackie" Maier after checking him out in the "Reborn" Kellett KD-1A in 1960. Maier was Kellett's Chief test pilot.   *(Howard Levy Photo)*

When the YG autogiros became surplus to the Air Corps, they were "bailed" out to the U.S. Border Patrol in Texas. (Note the "NC" number.) The craft had a civil certification as Kellett KD-1A.

(Alderic Tibault Photo)

A Kellett XR-3 bought from U.S. Army as surplus. This autogiro has "cyclic control" in its rotor operated by General Electric, Pilot A. W. Bayer.

(General Electric Photo)

Kellett XR-3 and B-24 bomber operated by General Electric in a research program. A. W. Bayer, Pilot.　*(General Electric Photo)*

TABLE OF AUTOGIRO MODELS & SPECIFICATIONS

YEAR	MFR	MODEL	SEATS	ENGINE	MODEL	HP	GROSS WT	EMPTY WT	ROTOR DIA	NO. BLADES
1928	Kellett	K-1-X	1	Szekley	—	40	1000	—	37	2
1930	Pitcairn	PCA-1	3	Wright	R-760-4	240	2750	—	43	4
1931	Pitcairn	PCA-2	3	Wright	R-760-4	240	3000	—	48	4
1931	Pitcairn	PCA-2	3	Wright	R-975/E	300	3000	2025	45	4
1931	Pitcairn	PCA-3	3	P&W	R-985	300	3063	2098	45	4
1931	Pitcairn	PAA-1	2	Kinner	B-5	125	1750	1178	37	4
1931	Pitcairn	PAA-2	2	Martin/Chev.	—	120	—	—	37	4
1931	Pitcairn	PA-18	2	Kinner	R-5	160	1950	1325	40	4
1931	Buhl	Pusher	2	Continental	R-670	165	1850	—	40	4
1932	Pitcairn	PA-19	5	Wright	R-975/E2	420	4640	2690	50'7½	4
1932	Pitcairn	PA-20	2	Kinner	B-5	125	1800	1178	37	4
1932	Pitcairn	PA-24	2	Kinner	R-5	160	1800	—	37	4
1932	Pitcairn	PA-21	3	Wright	R-975/E2	420	3000	—	45	4
1932	Kellett	K-2	2	Continental	R-670	160	2200	1556	—	4
1933	Kellett	K-3	2	Kinner	C-5	210	2300	1647	40'6"	4
1933	Pitcairn	PA-22	2	Pobjoy	Niagra	90	1140	600	32	3
1934	Kellett	K-4	2	Continental	R-670	210	2400	1620	40'6"	4
1935	Kellett	KD-1	2	Jacobs	L4MA7	225	2050	1345	40	3
1936	Kellett	YG-1A	2	Jacobs	L4MA7	225	2205	1586	40	3
1936	Pitcairn	PA-33	2	Wright	R-975/E2	420	3300	2300	46'2"	3
1936	Pitcairn	PA-34	2	Wright	R-975/E2	420	3300	2300	46'2	3
1937	Pitcairn	AC-35	2	Pobjoy	Niagra	90	1350	—	34'3½	3
1937	Kellett	YG-1B	2	Jacobs	L4MA7	225	2400	1617	40	3
1938	Pitcairn	PA-36	2	Warner	Super Scarab	165	2050	—	43	3
1939	G&A	PA-39	2	Warner	Super Scarab	165	2150	—	42'3	3
1939	Kellett	KD-1B	1	Jacobs	L4MA7	225	2295	1670	40	3
1939	Kellett	XR-2	2	Jacobs	R915-3	285	2400	—	40	3
1939	Kellett	XR-3	2	Jacobs	L4MA7	225	2250	—	40	3
1942	Kellett	XO-60	2	Jacobs	R-915-3	285	2640	—	43'2½	3
1942	G&A	XO-61	2	Jacobs	R-915-3	300	3038	—	48'	3

TABLE OF AUTOGIRO MODELS & SPECIFICATIONS (cont.)

DISC LOAD-G	WING SPAN	AREA	CRUISE SPEED	TOP SPEED	MIN SPEED	R.O.C.	
—	—	—	—	—	—	—	Never flown
1.8	33	90'.75	—	105	—	—	Geared engine "A" & "B" model 3-Blade magnes. prop.
1.6	30	88	—	110	—	—	Prototype
1.8	30	88	—	120	—	—	Also Navy XOP-1
1.8	30	88	—	120	—	—	Same as PCA-2 except eng.
1.6	22.9	61.6	—	—	—	—	
1.6	22.9	61.6	—	—	—	—	Same as PAA-1 except eng. Rotor pylon & no aux. fins.
1.5	21.3	55	80	100	—	680	
1.4	25'3	88'.5"	—	—	—	—	Used PA-18 rotor turning opposite direction
2.2	30'8	89.2	100	120	30	850	Cabin autogiro—5 built
1.7	22'9"	61.6	—	—	—	—	Similar to PAA-1 except had tail whl.
1.7	22'9"	61.6	—	—	—	—	Same as PAA-1 with 160 hp. eng.
1.8	30	88	—	—	—	—	Same as PCA-2 with 420 hp. Wright eng.
1.6	26	112	80	100	24	—	Side-by-side seating
1.8	26	112	93	110	24	1200	Similar to K-2 except engine
1.4	—	—	—	100	22	—	
1.8	24'7"	63	93	114	—	940	Refined K-3, one built, not certificated
1.6	—	—	100	120	16	1000	Direct control, no fixed wing folding blades
1.6	—	—	100	128	17	—	Similar to KD-1; KD-1A
1.3	—	—	115	140	22	—	Army YG-2 1 built to NACA
1.3	—	—	115	140	22	—	Navy XOP-2 same as YG-2 ex. l. gear
1.4	—	—	—	90	22	—	1 built for bureau of air commerce. Rear eng. rodable
1.8	—	—	103	128	17	—	Similar to KD-1A 9 built for U.S.A.F.
1.4	—	—	—	100	25	—	Metal fuselage—rear eng. steerable front whls 1 completed
1.5	—	—	—	93	22	—	7 rebuilt from PA-18 Direct Control—jump takeoff
1.7	—	—	100	130	22	—	Similar to KD-1A except 1 place, mail comp. front
1.8	—	—	—	120	—	—	YG-1B reworked w/jump takeoff
1.7	—	—	—	106	—	—	YG-1B reworked w/jump takeoff cyclic pitch & coll. pitch
1.4	—	—	—	127	—	—	Later—YO-60 7 built

It is certainly strange, perhaps uncanny, that although many inventors, designers and space-minded dreamers dreamed of and/or built various versions of fixed-wing, flapping-wing and powered rotating wing aircraft. Only one, Sr. Juan de la Cierva worked with the idea of unpowered rotating wings.

During the three decades, plus, that unpowered "autorotating wing" craft flew, the payload ranged from a few pounds to about 800 pounds.

They were used for lowering light cargo as unpiloted, unpowered craft. They were used for carrying payloads from the tops of buildings to the surface and vice-versa. They dispersed fungicides and other agricultural materials. They carried from one to five people on their unpowered rotating wings.

Early craft required a short run to become airborne if the flight was made with no wind. They suffered from control limitations because some minimal airspeed was needed to make their airplane-type controls function.

Early in the second decade, exact control of the craft at low or even zero airspeed was available. Vertical takeoffs to limited altitudes of 10 or 20 feet with unpowered rotors were routine. Through this no appreciable payload increase was offered.

The designers of helicopters, with powered rotors, quickly adopted the control systems used by these autorotating wing machines called AUTOGIROS. The helicopter, at this time gave great promise of flight completely independent of a prepared surface. In fact, in many cases, could perform their flight function of lifting and delivering their payload without taking off or landing on any surface. The transfer could be done while hovering above the lift or delivery point.

As helicopter brought utility, so came complexity. Powered rotors need full-time power-trains from the engine to the rotors. Single-rotor types induce torque from the rotor to the airframe and the fuselage wants to turn in the opposite direction from the rotor. To offset the torque an antitorque rotor at the tail is needed. When two helicopter rotors turn in opposite directions either laterally, in tandem or on a common axis the torque of one offsets the torque of the other adding even more complexity.

Autogiros, in forward flight climbed with added power, or descended with no power. The angle of incidence of their blades was permanently set at about 4 degrees. Regardless of what angle of attack the aircraft assumed, the blades remained at this angle and the blades *autorotated*.

To make helicopters ascend and to fly point-to-point, the rotor has to assume an 8 to 10 degree angle of incidence.

As long as the helicopter has power available it maintains the 8 to 10 degrees. If power is lost, the angle must be reduced to 4 or so degrees or the rotor will slow down and control is lost. With a reduced angle the rotor will continue to turn in *autorotation*. The craft must, of course descend, but it will be under control. It can land in an area not much larger than its rotor diameter.

Autogiros, except for the last few models, flew from takeoff to landing with a minimum angle of incidence built in the rotor.

Later models incorporated temporary incidence or pitch change for vertical takeoff and landing.

The helicopter can be flown at low speed that the fixed-wing craft cannot enjoy. The helicopter can hover, or descend at zero airspeed without risk of aerodynamically stalling the rotor.

The autogiro can be flown in each of these phases without rotor stall. Early autogiros, however, depended on fixed wing controls to guide them to a desired spot. When the airspeed dropped below 30 mph, control was nil.

The rotor was, however, inherently stable and could descend vertically at low airspeeds or zero airspeed without diverging from a steep glide or vertical approach.

To sum up these statements; the autogiro, at the end of its development could do all that the helicopter could do with an edge of safety, but could not hover.

To hover the helicopter must have its rotor driven constantly by some kind of powerplant. This requires a heavy and complex reduction gear system and in the case of the single-rotor craft, an antitorque rotor at the tail.

What would the future of the autogiro be, if it employed already-tried techniques? It could take off vertically, fly slowly, as low as zero mph and land vertically. Adding simple also-tried devices, could perform limited hovering with rotor tip drive jets. These do not require a gear reduction system. Driving the rotor at the tip does not impart a torque to the airframe as shaft-driven systems do.

There is no reason to believe that autogiros could not be built to carry payloads equal to the loads carried by the largest helicopters.

There are no reasons to believe that the rotor systems, single, dual lateral, tandem rotors could not be used on autogiros without heavy gear reduction systems.

Many ultra-light autogiros have been constructed as home-built projects and are being flown for pleasure or for limited business purposes.

New, lighter power plants, new airframe construction techniques; new better and lighter rotor systems, temporary drive systems such as torque converters; rotor tip drive with air driven by an engine driven compressor. In the thirties, engines ran small compressors which were used to start the engine. Autogiros could be designed with short wings for several purposes; part of the landing gear structure, to store fuel or light cargo and to accept some of the total lift in forward flight to relieve the rotor.

There is no apparent limit to the possibilities of the autogiro when some of the mentioned already-tried features are reapplied and some of the now-available techniques applied with modern concepts.

The Theory and a Discussion of the Autogiro

(Illustrations by Author.)

The AUTOGIRO literally flashed across the sky in the early twenties with Sr. Juan de la Cierva's craft making a successful flight in Spain on January 9, 1923. The rotor was turned by a phenomenon called "autorotation."

In about a twenty year flurry of activity, it seemed as though the autogiro was sent to make the helicopter, with which many inventors had labored for years and, years, a success. The helicopter interests had been trying since the latter part of the nineteenth century. The problems had been many, but two outstanding ones were power for flight and control in flight. With the arrival of the gasoline engine, the problem of power dissolved. Adequate control for such a machine that was intended to lift straight up and come straight down and fly with a great range of speed was not so easily solved.

By the early thirties the autogiro had a control system that used the rotating blades for control for vertical flight and at very low speeds.

About this time the clouds of World War II could be seen and the United States Military released a request for bids from aircraft manufacturers to design and build a helicopter.

Contracts were given to Sikorsky Aircraft in Bridgeport, Connecticut and Platt-LePage in the Philadelphia area.

In 1940, Sikorsky had a helicopter that could fly but the control system was so complicated that it was an impractical helicopter system to market.

Col. Frank Gregory, who was in charge of rotary wing design and procurement for the U.S. Air Corps, urged Sikorsky to enter into an agreement with the Autogiro Company of America as a licensee and thus have the use of all Autogiro Company's patents and designs. Sikorsky did this and with the autogiro rotor system added, had a very successful and relatively simple helicopter. Sikorsky began delivering helicopters to the United States Military in the early forties and with these deliveries, the autogiro activity effectively ceased. Without the work that the licensees of Cierva's principals in Europe and the work of licensees in the United States, success would not have come to the helicopter so quickly.

Autorotation was not invented by the helicopter engineers as a way to lower their crafts safely to the ground when their powerplant fails. Nor was it invented by Juan de la Cierva.

The force that makes autorotation possible was known to aeronautical inventors at least as far back as 1909. Nature has produced millions of tiny autorotating "craft" that deliver the maple seed to earth each year.

From a book titled *Practical Aeronautics* by Charles Hayward, copyright 1912; "*—constants used by Lielienthal show the arched surface (of an airfoil) still possess supporting powers when the angle of incidence becomes negative, i.e. below the horizontal. The air pressure becomes a propelling force at angles exceeding 3 degrees up to 30 degrees.*" So it can be seen that the scientists of those days knew of a forward propelling force.

A quote of an unknown author from the same book "*—by this construction, the air was thrust upward on the outer surface while the air rushed in to fill the partial vacuum thus formed, exerting a powerful lift at the same time was pushed forward, thus tending to diminish head resistance.*"

Later in the book, while discussing some soaring experiments by Octave Canute as early as 1909: "*—at certain angles, the total air pressure acting on the plane (wing) cease to act in a line normal to the plane (wing) or its chord, instead, the line of action of this force takes a position well in front. The pressure thus materially acting in the dual role of supporting and propelling force.*"

A "force diagram" from *Practical Aeronautics* (fig.1) shows the action of an airfoil in flight

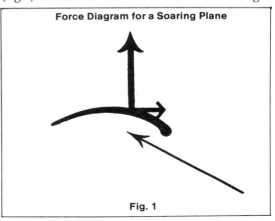

Force Diagram for a Soaring Plane

Fig. 1

showing one inventor's understanding of the forces: one vertical arrow, showing "lift" and another arrow *pointing forward* to illustrate the propelling force.

Messrs. Jackman and Russel, in the same book, referred to experiments with stuffed birds used as "flying models." "—*Thus we have a bird weighing 4.25 pounds, not only thoroughly supported,* but propelled forward by *a force of 0.359 pounds at 17 miles per hour.*" Other experiments discovered similar actions.

Figures 2, 3, and 4 try to explain the "rules" for lift, drag (resistance) and the forward propelling force.

Figure 2 shows the "rules":

1. Lift acts at *90 degrees* from the relative wind.
2. Drag acts *parallel* to the relative wind.

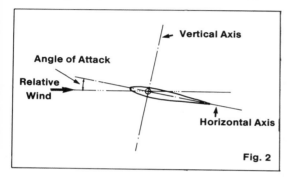

Fig. 2

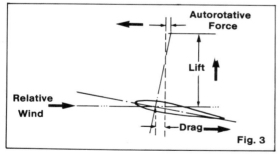

Fig. 3

With knowledge of this forward propelling phenomena it is easy to see that Cierva would decide to anchor one end of his airfoil(s) and when they were propelled forward, they would rotate.

In figure 3 it is assumed that the values of lift and drag, (measured in pounds) are drawn to the same scale. It can be seen that the "lift" line crosses the vertical axis of the airfoil. The value of the lift line ahead of the axis is a propulsive force. In figure 4, the angle of attack of the airfoil is increased which increases the drag. Lift is increased also, but not at the same rate as the drag. In this figure you will see that the "lift" line does not cross the vertical axis and no autorotative force is produced. In an actual situation,

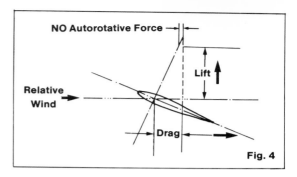

Fig. 4

very soon after the rotor was put in this angle of attack and if no power was being applied to the rotor, the rotation would stop.

Persons can usually understand that as long as the autogiro is in level flight, that the angle of attack will remain within the limits for producing an autotative force. Many never could, however, imagine how the angle of attack of the rotor blades could be kept at a low value when the autogiro was descending vertically, and the air is flowing straight up at the rotor.

Figure 5 shows that while the autogiro and the rotor system are descending vertically, usually at about 10 miles per hour, the rotor tip speed is about 200 miles an hour, and because it is in vertical descent, the air speed at the tip in any point around the circumferance of the rotor is the same and there is no "advancing" blade which meets a greater air speed for part of its circumference or a "retreating" blade which meets a wind blowing towards its trailing edge, because it is not in forward flight. It will be seen from figure 5 that a resolution of all the winds will show a resulting wind from a low enough angle to permit autorotation to continue.

Early in Cierva's experiments he discovered to his dismay that his rotorcraft rolled over on their sides as they began to leave the ground.

At this time, Cierva was solving another problem. He was concerned with the bending stresses on the rotor blades as the lift increased

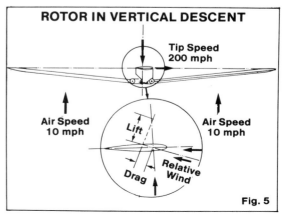

Fig. 5

145

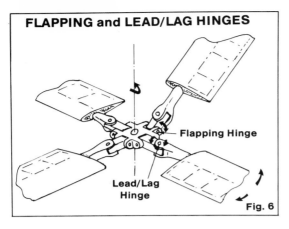

FLAPPING and LEAD/LAG HINGES

Flapping Hinge

Lead/Lag Hinge

Fig. 6

on one side of the rotating circle and decreased on the other.

Juan de la Cierva was a structural engineer and had in the past designed trusses for bridges that were pinned at the ends to permit motion at the ends to relieve bending.

Cierva never said that he "invented something" or that he "discovered something." He said, "God permitted (him) to know something."

He applied the bridge design principle to the autogiro rotor blade attachment at the hub. The pin at the hub permitted the blade to "flap" or rise and fall as it rotated (figure 6). When the blades were permitted to flap they not only relieved the bending, but allowed the additional lift on the "advancing" blade to cause the blade to rise, rather than roll the autogiro over. In this case, de la Cierva said "God permitted him to know two things." Cierva also put a vertical hinge on the blade to permit it to move fore and aft to relieve the bending as the drag increased on the "advancing" side and decreased on the "retreating" side.

In normal flight, the forward speed of the autogiro adds to the air speed passing over the

advancing blades and subtracts from the air speed that the retreating blades move in. As the blades advance, the increased air speed causes the blade to climb or "flap." As it does, it decreases its angle of attack (fig. 7). This action effectively equalizes the lift on each side of the rotor disc and permits the autogiro to fly level in forward flight instead of rolling because of the "unbalance of lift" across the rotor disc.

On the autogiros produced by Pitcairn and Kellett, the rotating mast of the rotor was inclined toward the retreating side and also inclined toward the rear, in that way "encouraging" the blades to flap (fig. 8-a & 8-b). To take care of the differences in lift that might be caused by this offset when the autogiro was descending vertically, a lead weight was bolted inside the tip of the right wing.

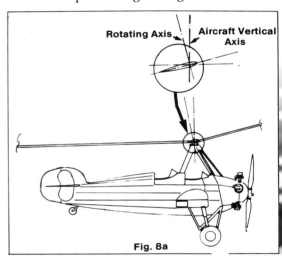

Rotating Axis — Aircraft Vertical Axis

Fig. 8a

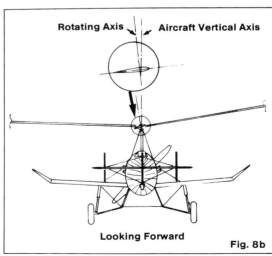

Rotating Axis — Aircraft Vertical Axis

Looking Forward

Fig. 8b

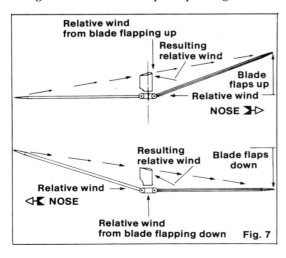

Relative wind from blade flapping up

Resulting relative wind

Blade flaps up

Relative wind

NOSE ➤

Resulting relative wind

Blade flaps down

Relative wind

◀ NOSE

Relative wind from blade flapping down

Fig. 7

In forward flight the blades of an autogiro are flapped up in the front and flapped down in the rear (fig. 9). The blades climb up from their low position at the tail to the high position at the

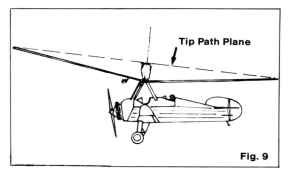

Tip Path Plane

Fig. 9

surfaces that were used on early autogiros could stall. When brought in for a landing, and the nose pulled up to reduce the contact speed, all control was lost. If the autogiro was too high when the flare was performed and the nose was not directly into the wind, the autogiro might begin to drift away from the wind. If this did happen and the autogiro contacted the ground in this altitude, the down-wind wheel would strike the ground sideways and the lift from the rotor, high above the wheel would cause the craft to roll over (fig. 10).

nose and descend back to the tail position. An imaginary line drawn from the tip of the most-forward blade to the tip of the rear-most blade would describe the blade tip position at any point in its rotation. This is called the "tip path plane" (fig. 9). It must be further understood that the air passes up through the rotor disc, unlike the downwash from a helicopter rotor.

Although the rotor could not stall, even when the autogiro is flying at very low airspeed or even zero airspeed, the airplane-type control

This was seen as a serious problem and the early pilots, who were professionals for the most part learned to avoid this condition. As more autogiros were manufactured and sportsmen pilots who might have had the same piloting experience, bought them an increase of these crosswind accidents occurred.

Cierva had begun his experiments with the rotor providing lateral control, but for some reason he abandoned it in favor of the airplane-

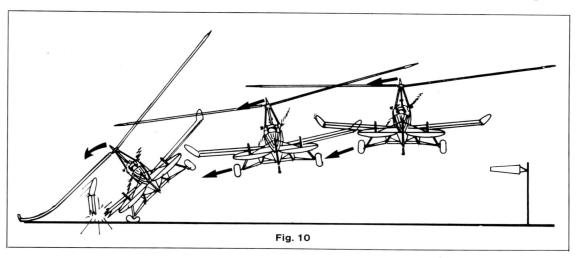

Fig. 10

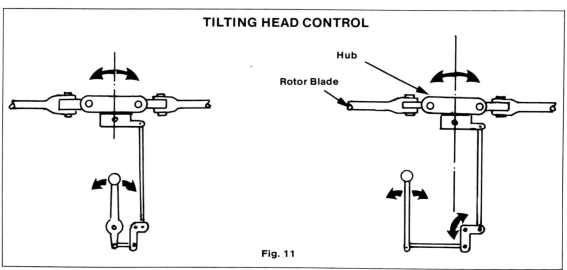

TILTING HEAD CONTROL

Hub

Rotor Blade

Fig. 11

type control surfaces. All the autogiros delivered in the United States from 1931 through 1934 had airplane type control surfaces.

Soon Cierva's Autogiros again were equipped with lateral control provided by the rotor and at the same time the rotor also controlled the autogiro longitudinally. All this was accomplished with a simple principle; tilting the rotating axis of the rotor in the direction that control was wanted. "Something for nothing" was too much to ask of the rotor; although the system was startlingly simple: —the control stick moved the rotor hub directly (fig. 11), through only one or two belcranks to provide the mechanical advantage so that the loads in the control stick were only a few pounds (fig. 12). The rotating part of the rotor system weighed about 300 pounds. With this mass spinning at 200 or more rpm, a powerful gyroscope was attached to the hand of the pilot. Any out-of-balance of the rotor, was fed back to the pilot's hand.

Any inflight disturbance was usually quickly dampened out by the rotor lead lag/dampers. But on the ground, during runup for takeoff or just after touchdown, it was an entirely different experience (fig. 13-a through f).

In figure 13-a, the rotor is stable because all three blades are equally spaced around the hub, 120 degrees apart.

In figure 13-b, the rotor pattern has been disturbed and two blades are closer to each other than they are to the remaining blade. Here you will see that although the C. G. of each blade has not changed, the collective C. G.'s of the two blades act against the remaining blade, with the collective C. G.'s at a new location and with their weights added together.

This tries to pull the rotor head toward the C.G. of the two blades, and because the landing gear tries to resist the autogiro rolling over, the tire compresses and the landing gear is compressed (fig. 13-b).

If the landing gear shock absorbing system (shock strut and tire) are not designed properly or not serviced properly, the reaction to their being compressed will try to push that side of the autogiro up at the same time the two blades that are closer together are on the opposite side of the autogiro.

The combination of the weight and C.G. shift and the landing gear reaction put a stronger force into the autogiro (fig. 13-c). This can, if the landing gear does not dampen it out, build up stronger and stronger with each revolution of the rotor until the autogiro rolls onto its side (fig. 13-f). The craft will also shake in a fore and aft direction, too, but because of the longer fore and aft stance the overturn will be to one side or the other. There are no certain number of oscillations until the autogiro upsets. If this happens on touchdown, the damage has been done before the pilot can react, and there is little he can do in any event. If it happens on runup, he has one chance; de-clutch the engine from the rotor drive and apply the rotor brake. This *might* cause all the blades to lag to the rear limit of their damper travel and they will be in an even spacing from each other. There is no record of this being successful. It is a theoretical practicality.

Figure 13 is not meant to imply that after the number of oscillations shown that the autogiro would overturn. Depending on a number of factors, it could happen in two or three or continue to rock without overturning. This unwanted activity is called "ground resonance" or "ground instability." It is never a problem with four-bladed autogiros because the four blades were wire braced to each other. It was difficult for the blades to get as close together as in the three-bladed systems. Removing the wings from autogiros when three-bladed rotors with control in the rotor came about, brought with it narrow landing gears that did not resist the rock-

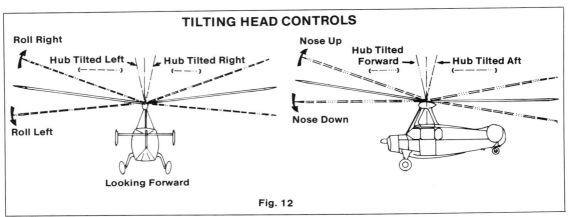

TILTING HEAD CONTROLS

Roll Right

Hub Tilted Left → | ← Hub Tilted Right
(— — — ·)   (— — ·)

Roll Left

Looking Forward

Nose Up

Hub Tilted
Forward → | ← Hub Tilted Aft
(— — ·)   (— — — ·)

Nose Down

Fig. 12

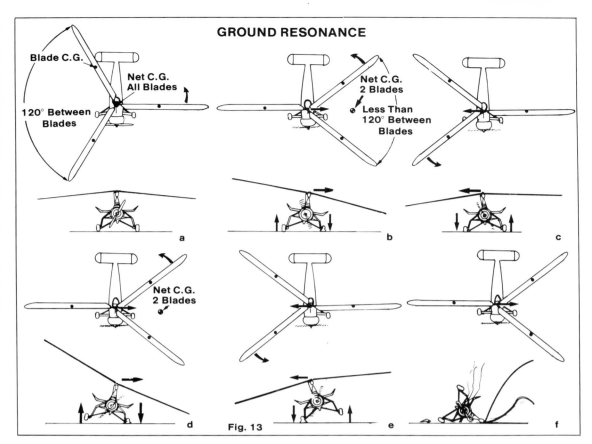

GROUND RESONANCE

Blade C.G.

Net C.G. All Blades

120° Between Blades

Net C.G. 2 Blades

Less Than 120° Between Blades

a

b

c

Net C.G. 2 Blades

d

Fig. 13

e

f

ing as well as the wide-stance gear on the four-bladed autogiros with wings. Neither does ground resonance usually occur with two-bladed craft because one blade always opposes only one blade.

Observers of the autogiro noticed that the propeller thrust line was tilted down (about five degrees) (fig. 14). Many surmised that this was done "to blow air on the rotor in order to keep it turning." The tilted engine caused the thrust line to pass through the C.G. of the autogiro which was unusually high because of the extra weight of the rotor system high above.

The three-bladed rotor system permitted two of the blades to be folded back alongside the third blade over the tail to make an ideal con-figuration for storage. The autogiro could then be towed behind a vehicle when the need arose. At times it might be more convenient or more economical to tow it.

To this point in its development the autogiro could cruise at about 100 to 110 miles per hour, when fixed-wing craft with the same horse-power were cruising at 120 mph. They could fly very slowly, as slow as 20 miles per hour and could land vertically with adequate control. It was still necessary, however, to make a short run of 20 to 50 feet to become airborne. To most persons it would have seemed logical to continue driving the rotor with the engine and take off vertically.

One of the main reasons this could not be

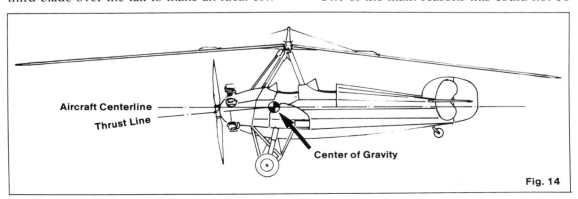

Aircraft Centerline

Thrust Line

Center of Gravity

Fig. 14

done was that while the rotor was being driven a torque was being imparted to the fuselage, with the weight of the autogiro on its wheel, the brakes could be used to prevent the rotor torque of the rotor from rotating the fuselage. If the autogiro rose into the air without some anti-torque device that would be effective in flight, the fuselage would rotate in the opposite direction as the rotor.

The second reason is that the incidence angle, or blade pitch, remained at about four degrees for all the autogiro's flight modes. This angle was not great enough for an efficient vertical flight even if the torque problem could be taken care of.

A solution was at hand, called "jump take-off." The autogiro could lift itself into the air without power in the rotor and could temporarily have an increase in the rotor blade which would be reduced once in the air.

The system was relatively simple. The blades were all set by the pilot at zero pitch or "no lift position" while the engine turned the rotor at about 150 percent of normal rpm. The rotor drive was quickly disconnected from the engine and simultaneously the rotor blade angle was increased to about 9 degrees. With the energy that was put into the rotor by overspeeding it, it continued to turn at a higher speed than normal with the blade angle at 9 degrees and the autogiro rose straight up to 5 or perhaps 20 feet, depending on the atmospheric conditions. As the rotor rpm slowed, the blade angle automatically returned to its 4 degree autorotative angle.

If one has ever played with one of those little toy propellers that were pushed up to a twisted flat metal strip by hand, you can see that the hand pushing the little propeller up the strip was the "power." As the propeller left the twisted strip, the power ceased and it continued to rise. This toy was not intended to autorotate and the steep angle of the blades soon spent all the energy in the propeller and it fell to the gound (unlike the autogiro).

The development of the autogiro came to a halt with the accomplishment of vertical takeoff, slow flight and vertical landing. Several "jump takeoff" autogiros were delivered to the military, but by this time the helicopter was an everyday flying machine.

The autogiro is still an excellent type of aircraft and perhaps some courageous developer will take it on.

Informative brochures and advetising of the autogiro in 1931 and 1932 by the Autogiro Company of America.
(Autogiro Company of America)

KELLETT AUTOGIRO
"Happy Landings"

No Landing Fields Needed
For the Autogiro.
Copyright, 1932, New York Evening Journal, Inc.   Registered U. S. Patent Office.

The solution of New York's problem as an air terminal was given the other day, in the opinion of many observers, by an autogiro which landed on a vacant city pier, picked up the inventor of the plane, the distinguished Spaniard, Juan de la Cierva, and took off a few minutes later for Floyd Bennett Field.

It was the first time that a passenger had ever flown in an airplane FROM Manhattan.

The landing and take-off were accomplished with nearly as much ease as a taxi drives up to the curb and then drives off. The autogiro hovered over the roofless pier at the foot of Spring St., pointed its nose into a strong west wind, and settled down vertically. It landed in the center of a circle of policemen, and did not roll ten inches.

About twenty feet were required for the take off. Then the plane soared into the air.

It seemed to be the answer to the question of city landing fields. The autogiro does not need any. And whether or not it becomes as popular for long distance flying as the ordinary plane, it should make an ideal "shuttle" for transferring city passengers to and from fields in the suburbs.

The time required to reach these fields now by ordinary methods of traffic is the worst obstacle to air travel. The autogiro eliminates it.

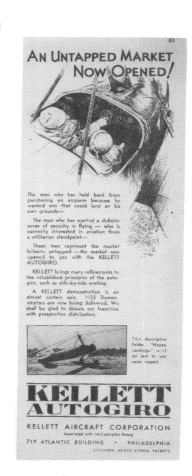

1960

SLOW and SURE

it lands in the length of its own **SHADOW**

the KELLETT
CROPMASTER

✔ **NO STALL POINT**

Fly as slow as 22 m.p.h., as low as needed to spot trouble or check on ground operations. No danger of falling into a spin from a stall, because moving air independently revolves the three-bladed rotor at all times, providing smooth, easy ascent or descent.

✔ **STANDARD POWER PLANT AND COCKPIT CONTROLS**

Plenty of power for any situation . . . at your fingertips. Conventional stick and rudder pedals provide natural control action. Special clutch applies auto-rotation power and automatically disengages.

✔ **NO MAINTENANCE PROBLEMS**

No special training required for your mechanics . . . plus advantage of standard spare parts inventory. You get more use, and more flying time by eliminating time lost to maintenance.

✔ **SAFETY ENGINEERED**

Designed into the Autogiro are integral safety factors which aerial applicators seek. The rugged rotor pylon acts as built-in pilot protection. Extra sturdy landing gear plus long-travel shock absorbers on both landing and tail wheels assure safe, easy landings on any terrain.

✔ **EASY STORAGE**

Rotor blades fold back for taxiing in confined areas, and permit storage in space only 10' x 10' x 26'.

✔ **SERVICE ANYWHERE**

Standard airplane maintenance. Wherever you land, any licensed A & E mechanic can work on this vehicle, using only the erection and maintenance manual.

KELLETT AUTOGIRO

"Happy Landings"

SAFE ~ EASY
"SLOW-MOTION"
LANDINGS

THE KELLETT AUTOGIRO

Kellett Autogiro advertising material emphasizing qualities and practical uses of the autogiro.

The AIRCRAFT
for the
PRIVATE
OWNER - FLYER

PITCAIRN
autogiro

Characteristics and features of
the 1932 Pitcairn Tandem

The Pitcairn Tandem is so named because of the arrangement of the cockpits, one behind the other. This gives full visibility to both passenger and pilot, and permits a design with less width which affords more speed per horse-power.

General specifications. Fuselage: Weight empty, 1310 lbs.; Gross weight, 1900 lbs.; Useful load, 590 lbs.; Length of Ship, 19 ft. 5 ins.; Span of Ship, 21 ft.; Wing area, 57.6 sq. ft.; Ground height (clearance to rotor hub), 10 ft. 6½ ins. Rotor: Diameter, 40 ft.; Blade area, 106.5 sq. ft.; Disc area, 1260 sq. ft. Power plant: Engine, 160 h.p.; Gasoline capacity, 30 gals.; Oil capacity, 3½ gals. Equipment: Combination pump and gravity fuel system with wobble pump; Dual controls; Motor starter; Cockpit primer; Metal propeller; Roller-bearing semi-low-pressure wheels; Parking brakes; Tail wheel and landing gear with Oleo shock absorbers; Fire extinguisher; Navigation lights; Leather upholstery; Safety glass windshields front and rear cockpits; Full complement of necessary instruments including compass; Cadmium plated fittings.

PITCAIRN AIRCRAFT, INC.
PITCAIRN FIELD, WILLOW GROVE, PA.

PITCAIRN
autogiro

PITCAIRN
Cabin Autogiro

THE ULTIMATE COMBINATION OF
SPEED, COMFORT AND SECURITY

Visiting among the skyscrapers

PITCAIRN
AUTOGIRO

*Making flyers
of you and me....*

PITCAIRN AIRCRAFT, INC.
PITCAIRN FIELD, WILLOW GROVE, PA.

Advertising material from Pitcairn Autogiro Company aimed at private owner-flyers showing cabin and a tandem passenger autogiros.

154

Pitcairn Autogiro Company brochure on construction and operating details for the Pitcairn Whirl Wing model.

... ANNOUNCING A NEW Pitcairn Autogiro, the *Whirl Wing*, which incorporates unique features of both design and construction. The flight performance of this new ship indicates that the fields of Autogiro use ... in civil, commercial and military aviation ... have been definitely widened.

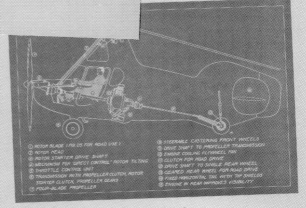

CONSTRUCTION AND OPERATING DETAILS ...

The Whirl Wing is the first Autogiro to have all-metal stressed-skin fuselage construction. The engine, a Warner Super-Scarab of 175 hp., is located within the center of the ship, with an insulated metal bulkhead between the cabin and the motor compartment. The main power shaft runs forward in a housing between the seats to the transmission unit within the nose of the fuselage. A small power shaft runs from the rear of the engine to drive the rear wheel for roadability.

The rotor hub on the Whirl Wing is radically new. It provides perfectly smooth operation of the rotor and virtually eliminates the transmission of any rough or disturbing forces from the rotor system to the pilot's control wheel. In this new hub the flapping hinges are at a 60° (instead of a 90°) angle to the rotor blade axes, which provide an automatic aerodynamic cushioning or "feathering" of the blades in flight. The axes of the flapping hinges are located close to the vertical rotor axis and, also, the center about which the rotor-control movements take place is practically in the plane of the rotor. Consequently, control loads are pleasingly light under all flight conditions.

The jump take-off is operated by a hydraulic system and is actuated by a single handle which simultaneously locks the wheel brakes, sets the rotor blades at zero pitch and engages the clutch of the rotor drive shaft. After the throttle has been advanced to full power and

the rotor reaches a speed of about 300 r.p.m., the mere turning of the single control handle causes the ship to rise vertically into flight.

The transmission in the forward end of the ship contains a variable gear reduction to the propeller. It automatically changes the speed of the propeller from 2 to 1 ratio during the period of rotor acceleration to a higher propeller speed at the time of take-off and subsequent flight. It also incorporates the clutch mechanism for transmitting power to build up the rotor speed while the ship is on the ground. Like all Autogiros, no power is applied to the rotor while the ship is in flight.

Flight control of the Whirl Wing is accomplished with the normal airplane hand wheel and foot pedals. The wheel controls the lateral and longitudinal movement of the rotor axis and the pedals are connected to a vertical rudder on the tail. On the ground these same pedals are used to steer the landing wheels.

The cabin appointments, instruments and controls in the Whirl Wing have been designed and arranged with the simplicity of modern automotive practice. Stewart Warner instrument panel, Ross automotive steering units. Electric Autolite ignition, and similar standard components have been adapted for use in this ship.

PITCAIRN AUTOGIRO COMPANY

WILLOW GROVE • PENNSYLVANIA

155

A Glossary of Autogiro Terms

Advancing Blade The blade that is moving into the oncoming airstream caused by forward flight of the aircraft.

Airfoil (Rotor) The profile of the rotor blade that would be present if the blade was sliced through from leading edge to trailing edge.

Angle of Attack The angle made by the intersection of a line drawn parallel with the chord line of the rotor airfoil and a line drawn parallel with the relative wind.

Angle of Incidence The angle made by the intersection of a line parallel with the chordline of the rotor airfoil and the horizontal (flapping) pin.

Area (Blade) The actual area, in square feet included within the airfoil section of one blade, not including blade attach fittings and devices.

Area (Rotor) The area in square feet included within a circle drawn using the length of one blade from center of rotation to the tip, as the radius.

Autogiro When spelled with a capital "A" denotes an aircraft, supported in flight by a rotor which is turning by the principle of autorotation, and produced by Sr. Juan de la Cierva or one of his licensees. When spelled with a lower case "a" it is intended to mean an autogiro-type aircraft built by persons other than Cierva licensees.

Blade (Rotor) One of the elements in a rotor system that produces lift (in early days called rotor vanes).

Blade Track The actual tip path of all blades in a rotor system.

Blade Tracking The adjusting of the flight of each blade in the rotor system so that each blade follows the same path for smooth flight.

Camber The top and bottom curvature of an airfoil.

Center of Gravity (Chordwise C.G.) The distance, in inches and hundredths of an inch, from the leading edge of a rotor blade at which the blade would balance chordwise.

Center of Gravity (Spanwise G.G.) The distance, in inches and hundredths of an inch from the center of rotation toward the tip, at a point where the blade would balance spanwise.

Chord Line (Horizontal Axis) A line running from the leading edge of an airfoil to the trailing edge.

Coning Angle The flapping angle that the blade assumes as it revolves into the relative wind and with the relative wind. There is no mechanical stop to limit the up-flapping of the blades. The centrifugal force tries to pull the blade away from the center of rotation and lift tries to raise the blade straight up. The combination of the lifting force and centrifugal force causes the blade to have an angle above the horizontal.

Damper Lead-Lag A mechanical device that restricts the lead-lag motion of a rotor blade. Usually a viscous or friction method. The stationary part may be attached to the hub. The active part to the blades.

Diameter (Rotor)	A great circle using as the radius the length of one blade in the system from the center of rotation.
Disc Loading	The percentage of the design gross weight carried on each square foot of the rotor "disc" area expressed in pounds per square foot.
Drag	An aerodynamic force that resists the motion of objects being moved through the air. As the speed of the air over the object increases or the speed of the object increases through the air.
Droop Cable	The older, 1920–1930's autogiro supported the blades while on the ground or at low rotational speeds with a cable attached to the blade about 1/3 of the distance out from the hub and to a "cone" or "tower" on the center of rotation.
Droop Stop	A positive mechanical stop to restrict the down-flapping of the rotor blade on autogiros that weren't equipped with droop cables.
Flapping Hinge	The mechanical joint including the flapping or horizontal pin which permits the freedom of motion for the blade tip to move up and down.
Flapping Link	An attachment between the inboard (root) end of the rotor blade and the hub. The inboard end receives the flapping pin. The outboard end usually has the accommodation for the lead/lag pin.
Ground Resonance (Ground Instability)	An undesirable dynamic condition that usually happens in three blade rotor systems that have shock absorbing landing gear and/or pneumatic tires, with lead/lag hinges in their rotor systems.
Gyrocopter	A proprietary name belonging to Dr. Igor Bensen and describing autorotating rotary wing aircraft constructed by him or constructed from kits or from parts supplied by him. The craft may be a motorless towed glider type or a powered craft.
Gyroplane	A rotary wing craft which may or may not resemble the autogiro type.
Hub (Rotor)	The element at the center of rotation of the rotor to which the blades are attached.
Interblade Cables	Early 1920, 1930's autogiros had lead-lag dampers installed in the blades a bit more that 1/3 of the distance from the center of rotation to the tip. Cables connected the damper actuating arm from one blade to the next.
Jump Takeoff	A vertical takeoff made by temporarily increasing the incidence of all blades in the rotor system simultaneously. The autogiro rises straight up, 5 to 20 feet; the incidence is reduced to normal and the autogiro flies away. No mechanical power is used to make the jump.
Lead-Lag Hinge	The mechanical joint, including the lead-lag pin which would permit the freedom of motion for the blade tip to move forward or backward.
Power Loading	Calculated same as a fixed wing type by dividing the design gross weight by the horsepower expressed in pounds per horsepower.
Retreating Blade	The blade that is moving **with** the oncoming airstream caused by the forward flight of the aircraft.

Retreating Blade Stall
Aerodynamic stalling of a rotor blade as it turns from nose to tail. This is caused when the forward speed of the aircraft is high enough that when this air speed is subtracted from the air speed caused by the rotation of the blade, the relative wind speed on the retreating side is so low that not enough lift is created on that side of the aircraft. The aircraft will roll to the retreating blade side; pitch up or both.

Running Takeoff
A takeoff made with the rotor prerotated to nearly cruising RPM while moving forward at full throttle.

Solidity Ratio
The ratio of the total actual area of all blades in a rotor system to the total rotor area; expressed in percent.

Shear Pin
A pin made from soft metal or with a hole thorough its length or grooves cut around it or all these things to limit the power delivered to the rotor during prerotation. The pin will shear and interrupt the power train if more than design horsepower was applied to the prerotation drive system.

Taxi Takeoff
A takeoff made without the aid of a prerotating mechanism during which the rotor speed is brought up to takeoff speed by taxiing the craft along the ground while slowly and carefully increasing the taxi speed as the rotor speed increases because of autorotative force.

Tip Path Plane
An imaginary straight line connecting the tips of all blades when viewed from front, rear or either side.

Tip Speed
The speed of the tip of the rotor blades of a rotor craft, usually expressed in feet per second.

Tilting Head
A rotor system in which the hub of the rotor system and all blades may be moved so that the rotating axis could be tilted fore and aft and side to side to accomplish lateral and longitudinal control. A normal control stick furnished the motion.

Wing Loading
Calculated same as a fixed-wing type by dividing the design gross weight by the wing area (if a wing was used) expressed in pounds per square foot.

LIST OF ILLUSTRATIONS

INDEX

478 03\05 20
42183   BUI